Deformable Surface 3D Reconstruction from Monocular Images

Synthesis Lectures on Computer Vision

Editors

Gérard Medioni, *University of Southern California*
Sven Dickinson, *University of Toronto*

Synthesis Lectures on Computer Vision publishes 50- to 150 page publications on topics pertaining to computer vision and pattern recognition. The scope largely follows the purview of premier computer science conferences, such as ICCV, CVPR, and ECCV.

Deformable Surface 3D Reconstruction from Monocular Images
Mathieu Salzmann and Pascal Fua
2010

Boosting-Based Face Detection and Adaptation
Cha Zhang, Zhengyou Zhang
2010

Image-Based Modeling of Plants and Trees
Sing Bing Kang, Long Quan
2009

Deformable Surface 3D Reconstruction from Monocular Images

Mathieu Salzmann and Pascal Fua

ISBN: 978-3-031-00682-1   paperback
ISBN: 978-3-031-01810-7   ebook

DOI 10.1007/978-3-031-01810-7

A Publication in the Springer series
SYNTHESIS LECTURES ON COMPUTER VISION

Lecture #3
Series Editors: Gérard Medioni, *University of Southern California*
                Sven Dickinson, *University of Toronto*
Series ISSN
Synthesis Lectures on Computer Vision
Print 2153-1056   Electronic 2153-1064

Deformable Surface 3D Reconstruction from Monocular Images

Mathieu Salzmann
Toyota Technological Institute at Chicago

Pascal Fua
École Polytechnique Fédérale de Lausanne

SYNTHESIS LECTURES ON COMPUTER VISION #3

ABSTRACT

Being able to recover the shape of 3D deformable surfaces from a single video stream would make it possible to field reconstruction systems that run on widely available hardware without requiring specialized devices. However, because many different 3D shapes can have virtually the same projection, such monocular shape recovery is inherently ambiguous.

In this survey, we will review the two main classes of techniques that have proved most effective so far: The template-based methods that rely on establishing correspondences with a reference image in which the shape is already known, and non-rigid structure-from-motion techniques that exploit points tracked across the sequences to reconstruct a completely unknown shape. In both cases, we will formalize the approach, discuss its inherent ambiguities, and present the practical solutions that have been proposed to resolve them. To conclude, we will suggest directions for future research.

KEYWORDS

computer vision, deformable surfaces, monocular 3D shape recovery, structure from motion

Contents

Acknowledgments

Parts of the authors' work described in this book was supported by grants from the Swiss National Science Foundation.

We also wish to acknowledge the invaluable help from many present and former colleagues from EPFL's Computer Vision Laboratory. We are especially indebted to Slobodan Ilic, Vincent Lepetit, Francesc Moreno-Noguer, Raquel Urtasun, and Aydin Varol.

Mathieu Salzmann and Pascal Fua
December 2010

Figure Credits

Figure 1.1   J. Pilet, V. Lepetit, and P. Fua. Fast Non-Rigid Surface Detection, Registration and Realistic Augmentation. *International Journal of Computer Vision*, 76(2), February 2008. With kind permission from Springer Science+Business Media, Copyright © 2008 Springer. DOI: 10.1007/s11263-006-0017-9

1.2   K. S. Bhat, C. D. Twigg, J. K. Hodgins, P. K. Khosla, Z. Popovic, and S. M. Seitz. Estimating Cloth Simulation Parameters from Video. In *ACM Symposium on Computer Animation*, 2003. Copyright (c) 2003, Association for Computing Machinery, Inc. Reprinted by permission.

1.4   Courtesy of Mingxing Hu.

1.5   M. Salzmann, F. Moreno-Noguer, V. Lepetit, and P. Fua. Closed-Form Solution to Non-Rigid 3D Surface Registration. In *European Conference on Computer Vision*, October 2008. DOI: 10.1007/978-3-540-88693-8_43

2.1   V. Blanz and T. Vetter. A Morphable Model for the Synthesis of 3D Faces. In *ACM SIGGRAPH*, pages 187–194, August 1999. Copyright © 1999, Association for Computing Machinery, Inc. Reprinted by permission.

2.2   M. Dimitrijević, S. Ilić, and P. Fua. Accurate Face Models from Uncalibrated and Ill-Lit Video Sequences. In *Conference on Computer Vision and Pattern Recognition*, June 2004. Copyright © 2004 IEEE. Used with permission. DOI: 10.1109/CVPR.2004.26

4.2-4.4   M. Salzmann, R. Hartley, and P. Fua. Convex Optimization for Deformable Surface 3D Tracking. In *International Conference on Computer Vision*, October 2007. Copyright © 2007 IEEE. Used with permission. DOI: 10.1109/ICCV.2007.4409031

4.6   M. Perriollat and A. Bartoli. A Quasi-Minimal Model for Paper-Like Surfaces. In *BenCos: Workshop Towards Benchmarking Automated Calibration, Orientation and Surface Reconstruction from Images*, 2007. Copyright © 2007 IEEE. Used with permission. DOI: 10.1109/CVPR.2007.383356

CHAPTER 1

Introduction

Deformable surface 3D reconstruction from monocular images is an active area of research in the Computer Vision community. This encompasses recovering both the shape of thin objects that can be treated as surfaces without perceptible thickness and the visible envelope of fully 3D objects. Whereas this may seem easy for a human being, it remains a challenging and ambiguous problem for computer-based techniques. This is especially true when the sensor data is noisy, which is typically the case when dealing with real images.

Apart from being a fascinating problem, non-rigid 3D shape recovery has applications in many different domains:

- The entertainment industry could benefit greatly from improved techniques for video-based shape recovery. In animation movies, video games, or special effects, many things are still done manually, image after image. As illustrated by Fig. 1.1, there are already effective techniques for handling 2D surface deformations in an Augmented Reality context. However, they must be extended to full 3D deformations to better account for phenomena such as self-occlusion and self-collisions that become prevalent as the deformations become larger. This could be used to draw virtual advertisement logos on athletes' or fashion models' clothes, thus avoiding the need to physically print them and making it easy to change them as necessity dictates. Similarly, a lot of time could be saved if the deformations of the clothes of animated characters, such as those of Fig. 1.2, could simply be obtained by filming a real person performing some motion, reconstructing his or her clothes in 3D, and re-applying the resulting deformations to the animated character.

- Many sports could benefit from a system that reconstructs non-rigid 3D shapes from video. For example, as shown in Fig. 1.3 (a,b), sailors want to analyze the effect of their maneuvers on the shape of their sails, or, sometimes even more interestingly, study the sails of their opponents. In this context, video presents a clear advantage over other sensors that should be placed on the sail itself, thus changing its behavior. Similarly, analyzing the deformations of any sports structure, such as the skis or the plane wings of Fig. 1.3 (c,d), in realistic situations could help improving their design.

- More speculatively, in the medical field, the current trend is to make surgery ever less invasive. This implies smaller and smaller cuts in the patient's skin, which do not give the surgeons a direct view of their work. They only leave enough space for small cameras to be introduced into the patient's body. In such conditions, the resulting images are of poor quality, and make

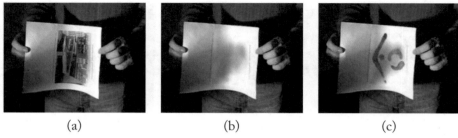

(a)   (b)   (c)

Figure 1.1: Augmented Reality. (a) A deformed piece of paper. (b) The illustration has been virtually removed. (c) It has been replaced by the properly deformed and reshaded logo of a conference Pilet *et al.* [2008].

knit   linen   fleece   satin

Figure 1.2: The entertainment industry could use 3D reconstruction from video for different applications. For example, animating the cloth of virtual characters could be guided by video, thus limiting manual intervention Bhat *et al.* [2003]. Courtesy of K. Bhat.

the surgeons' work much harder. As shown in Fig. 1.4, having a full 3D representation of the organ's surface recovered from the images, or an augmented view of the organs, would be of great use. In particular, it could help the surgeons orient themselves more easily and improve their perception of where their tools are with respect to the relevant surfaces.

In all these cases, using more than one camera greatly simplifies matters by allowing the use of multi-view stereo techniques. Consequently, there has been increasing interest in relying on stereo to recover the complex shapes of clothes Starck and Hilton [2007]. This constitutes a very hard application, since the folds and wrinkles of clothing produce many self-occlusions, and make simple matching techniques fail. Various matching techniques have been proposed, such as spherical matching Starck and Hilton [2005], as well as different shape representations such as Laplacian surfaces de Aguiar *et al.* [2007]. The resulting motion capture techniques have been successfully applied with specific markers printed on the garments White *et al.* [2007], and, more recently, without any such markers Bradley *et al.* [2008]. However, using multiple cameras also makes the deployment of the corresponding system much harder since the cameras have to be synchronized and

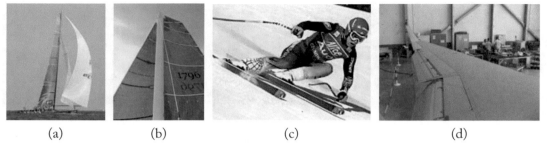

| (a) | (b) | (c) | (d) |

Figure 1.3: Many sports design tasks could benefit from 3D shape recovery. (a,b) Sailors are interested in knowing the shape of their own sails and that of their opponents. (c,d) Recovering the true deformations of skis during a race or of a wing in flight could help improve their design.

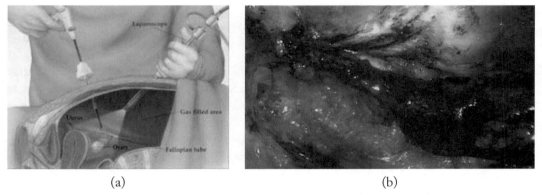

| (a) | (b) |

Figure 1.4: Surface reconstruction applied to medical imaging. (a) Schematic representation of non-invasive surgery. (b) Image acquired during endoscopic coronary artery bypass surgery using the da Vinci robotic system. Courtesy of Mingxing Hu.

calibrated. The multiple cameras can be replaced by a structured-light projector that can be bundled together with a single camera Microsoft [2010]. This can produce very reliable depth-maps in real-time but has limited range and cannot exploit ordinary video footage. Alternatively, photometric stereo Hernandez *et al.* [2007], Hertzmann and Seitz [2003], Woodham [1980] could be employed to reconstruct deformable surfaces by using several images taken under different lighting conditions. This technique is very reliable and yields outstanding results, but, as multiview-stereo, it requires an elaborate setup and is not well adapted to capturing rapidly deforming shapes. From a practical standpoint, there is therefore a strong incentive for achieving this kind of reconstruction from a single video stream.

Unfortunately, recovering the 3D shape of surfaces such as those shown in Fig. 1.5 from a single video-stream is an ill-constrained problem. The high number of parameters and the noisy image information make it impractical to solve without prior knowledge of the possible deformations that

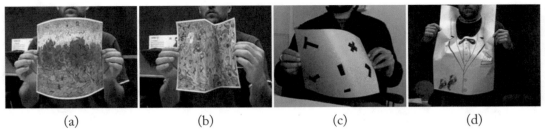

| (a) | (b) | (c) | (d) |

Figure 1.5: Examples of deformed surfaces. (a) Textured and developable surface undergoing a simple deformation. Its 3D shape can be recovered using many existing approaches that rely either on textural or edge information. (b) Here, the sharp creases would result in failure of techniques that rely heavily on geometric smoothness. (c,d) With much less textured surfaces whose contours may be partially occluded, the shape of uniform parts must be inferred from that of the textured ones. This requires deformation models that accurately represent the properties of the surfaces, or the ability to use additional cues, such as shading.

the surface can undergo. All successful approaches to this problem exploit the fact that real surfaces do not deform randomly and cannot assume completely irrational shapes. As a consequence, one may introduce some knowledge of what is feasible and what is not to constrain the recovery and resolve the ambiguities.

In this survey, we will therefore introduce a number of state-of-the-art methods that address these issues. More specifically, we will first review the techniques that have been proposed over the years to model the deformations of non-rigid surfaces. We will discuss their strengths and weaknesses for monocular 3D shape recovery purposes and will introduce two more recent classes of techniques that have been designed to overcome these weaknesses. The first includes template-based approaches that rely on establishing correspondences with a reference image in which the shape is known *a priori*. The second comprises structure-from-motion algorithms that are template-free but require points to be tracked across video sequences. For both classes, we will first formalize the problem and its inherent ambiguities. We will then describe the various methods that have been introduced to overcome them. Finally, we will conclude with some perspectives on potential avenues of research to extend the scope of all these techniques and to take them from the laboratory into the real world.

CHAPTER 2

Early Approaches to Non-Rigid Reconstruction

Modeling the behavior of non-rigid surfaces has been an active area of research for the past twenty years. Many approaches have been proposed in the context of both Computer Vision and Computer Graphics. These two fields are closely related, since Computer Vision aims at solving the inverse problem of Computer Graphics, that is recovering the shape of real objects as opposed to simulating the deformations of virtual ones. It is therefore not surprising that similar representations often appear in both domains.

Throughout the years, approaches to non-rigid surface reconstruction have relied on many different techniques to represent and constrain surface deformations. These techniques can be roughly classified into those that are physics-based, rely on statistical learning methods, or parameterize the shape to implicitly regularize its deformations.

Some of them have proved very successful for their intended purposes but not necessarily for generic monocular 3D surface reconstruction. In this chapter, we briefly review these techniques. We discuss their strengths, that the more recent methods described in the remainder of this survey exploit, and their weaknesses that these same methods attempt to correct.

2.1 PHYSICS-BASED MODELS

In both the Computer Vision and Computer Graphics fields, most early approaches to modeling deformations of non-rigid objects were inspired by Mechanical Engineering concepts. The key idea was to model the behavior of an object by describing the true physical laws that govern it. A seminal work in this field Kass et al. [1988] advocated using this approach to delineate 2D image shapes and was quickly extended to 3D modeling Terzopoulos et al. [1987, 1988]. In the proposed formalism, a global energy, written as the sum of an internal one and an external one, is minimized. The internal energy derives from physical surface properties and typically acts as a regularizer that enforces global smoothness. It is often taken to be quadratic to convexify the minimization problem and make its resolution simpler. The external energy encodes the image information and allows image features to act as attraction forces that tend to deform the surface to make it conform to these features.

The formulation introduced in Kass et al. [1988] and many of the subsequent methods Fua [1996] are directly inspired by Mechanical Engineering techniques, especially the Finite Element Method (FEM) Bathe [1982], Zienkiewicz [1989]. In the remainder of this section, we briefly introduce FEM. We then discuss why it is too complex to be used in its complete form in either

Computer Graphics or Computer Vision applications and introduce some of the simplified versions that have proved effective in these fields.

2.1.1 THE FINITE ELEMENT METHOD

FEM Bathe [1982], Zienkiewicz [1989] is the method of choice to accurately simulate the deformations of structures such as beams, plates, shells, and 3D volumes under various loads. The structure of interest is represented by a discrete set of elements, such as segments, triangles, or tetrahedra, that are linked by their nodes. Following the laws of mechanics, mass, damping, and stiffness matrices are built for each element separately. These matrices typically depend on physical parameters, such as Young's modulus, Poisson's ratio, shear modulus, and thickness of the structure. They are then assembled to write the equations of motion that govern the deformations of the whole structure as

$$\mathbf{M\ddot{u}} + \mathbf{D\dot{u}} + \mathbf{Ku} = \mathbf{f} , \tag{2.1}$$

where $\mathbf{u}$ is the unknown vertex displacement, $\mathbf{M}$, $\mathbf{D}$, and $\mathbf{K}$ are the mass, damping, and stiffness matrices respectively, and $\mathbf{f}$ represents the external forces. This models the full dynamical behavior, which can be simplified by ignoring the terms depending on temporal derivatives when only attempting to compute static deformations.

When considering only small deformations of a materially linear object, that is deformations that are only barely visible, the matrices of Eq. 2.1 can be assumed to be independent of the deformation, and the system can be solved directly. However, almost by definition, both Computer Vision and Computer Graphics are concerned by much larger deformations that are clearly visible. This introduces geometrical nonlinearities that can be compounded with the fact that the material may be subject to either hyper-elasticity or plasticity phenomena. Consequently, the stiffness matrices become functions of the displacements, and the whole problem becomes much more complex because they have to be recomputed very often. This results not only in an additional computational burden but often also in instabilities due to buckling or the appearance of critical points that yield different solutions.

Many resolution methods have been proposed over the years to overcome these difficulties. The best known ones are the following Zienkiewicz [1989]:

- **The Total Lagrangian approach.** The solution is computed from a reference configuration that remains unchanged throughout the computation.

- **The Updated Lagrangian approach.** It operates along the same lines as the Total Lagrangian approach, except for the fact that the reference configuration is replaced by the current solution every so often.

- **The Corotational Approach.** It involves decomposing large deformations into rigid transformations of the elements and small deformations, which allows for stable resolution.

The last two are the most commonly used today. They are successful in Mechanical Engineering but require both tremendous computational power, which makes them ill-suited for real-time Computer

Graphics applications, and a precise knowledge of the physical properties of the surfaces being modeled, which is only rarely available to Computer Vision applications. Consequently, in both fields, a lot of effort has gone into simplifying these approaches to the point where they become practical in their respective contexts. Below, we distinguish between the methods used in Computer Graphics and in Computer Vision.

2.1.2   PHYSICS-BASED METHODS FOR COMPUTER GRAPHICS

A key driver behind the use of physics-based models in Computer Graphics has been the need to model the deformations of clothes House and Breen [2000], preferably in real-time. In the absence of good deformation models, artists must manually design the shape of the virtual characters' garments in each frame of a sequence. Physics-based models both constrain the feasible deformations and make animation much easier. Several cloth models have been proposed, ranging from early versions Ng and Grimsdale [1996], Volino et al. [1995] that only achieved visually plausible results to much more physically-accurate and realistic ones Bridson et al. [2002, 2003].

While physics-based approaches produce good results, they typically yield computationally expensive solutions. Therefore, there have been many attempts at improving the speed and robustness of the solvers Volino and Magnenat-Thalmann [2001]. For example, to overcome the perennial problem that very small time steps have to be taken to avoid numerical instabilities, implicit time integration was introduced Baraff and Witkin [1998]. Another example is the use of the Boundary Element Method James and Pai [1999], an alternative to FEM where the original differential equations are replaced by integral equations over the boundary of the object, to speedup the simulations.

In addition to improving the resolution speed, more accurate nonlinear FEM was also studied in Computer Graphics. This was done in particular for surgery simulation purposes Picinbono et al. [2000], and for general deformable objects modeling Barbič and James [2005], Hirota et al. [2000], Wu et al. [2001]. The corotational approach proved succesful in this context of large deformations Hauth and Strasser [2004], Müller et al. [2002], as well as other representations such as discrete shells Grinspun et al. [2003], or invertible finite elements Irving et al. [2004]. Accurate nonlinear representations being very complex, simplifications have been proposed to yield physically plausible deformations based on elastically coupled rigid cells Botsch et al. [2007].

Finally, while advances in Mechanical Engineering have resulted in improved Computer Graphics methods, the process sometimes also went the other way. Subdivision surfaces Catmull and Clark [1978], Doo and Sabin [1978], already well-known in the Graphics community, were introduced to the Mechanical Engineering community in the context of finite elements. They involve representing a surface with a coarse mesh, which can then be refined following a subdivision scheme Loop [1987]. This reduced the complexity of the finite element models, thus yielding more efficient representations Cirak et al. [2000].

2.1.3 PHYSICS-BASED METHODS FOR COMPUTER VISION

As they became very popular in Computer Graphics for simulation and animation purposes, physics-based models also gained acceptance in Computer Vision for non-rigid motion analysis Kambhamettu *et al.* [1994]. In both fields, their main purpose was to restrict the potential deformations of an object to plausible ones only. However, in Computer Graphics where the simulation results have to look realistic, physical accuracy, or at least plausibility, is more important than in Computer Vision. There, the main concern is quality of fit to image data and robustness to erroneous measurements. The role of the model is that of a regularizer that turns the model fitting process into one that is easier to perform.

The original Snakes Kass *et al.* [1988] are a good example of this. The external energy that serves as a regularizer is written as a quadratic function that approximates the sum of the square of the curvatures along the surface, which itself is an approximation of the true elastic deformation energy. The fact that it is not a particularly accurate approximation of the true energy is more than made up by the fact that it can be expressed in quadratic form, thereby allowing a very effective semi-implicit optimization scheme. The same formulation was later extended to 2D shape recovery Pilet *et al.* [2008] and 3D surface modeling from stereo Fua and Leclerc [1995] using triangulated meshes.

Many other variations of the physics-based models have been proposed since to reconstruct surfaces from images. In the medical imaging domain, *balloon forces* Cohen and Cohen [1993] were introduced to make the surface expand from its initial state so that it could be started from inside the object to be outlined. Deformable superquadrics Metaxas and Terzopoulos [1993], Terzopoulos and Metaxas [1991] were proposed to reconstruct more complex shapes by modeling both global and local deformations. Finally, in McInerney and Terzopoulos [1993, 1995], the FEM formulation was followed more closely, and a deformable surface was modeled as a thin-plate under tension. More recently, the use of the Boundary Element Method has also been advocated to track deformable objects in 2D Greminger and Nelson [2003] and in 3D Greminger and Nelson [2008]. Comparisons of these different FEM formulations are available both specifically for medical imaging McInerney and Terzopoulos [1996] and in a broader context Montagnat *et al.* [2001].

There has been some interest in more accurate modeling of the true physics of deformable objects via the nonlinear finite element method in Computer Vision. However, unlike in Computer Graphics where one can tune the forces and material parameters until satisfactory deformations are produced, recovering surface shape by fitting a model to the image data requires these parameters to be fixed during the optimization process. Some approaches that rely on sophisticated models have nonetheless been proposed for fitting a mesh to 3D range data Huang *et al.* [1995], Jojic and Huang [1997], Tsap *et al.* [1998] and for video-based shape recovery Bhat *et al.* [2003], Tsap *et al.* [2000]. They involve an analysis-by-synthesis approach and a more-or-less exhaustive search through the parameter space until those that yield the best fit are found. Recently a nonlinear FEM formulation Ilić and Fua [2007] has been proposed to recover the deformations of beam structures in the image plane, where image features act as forces, as in the original Snakes Kass *et al.* [1988]. To the best of our knowledge no similar nonlinear model has yet been used in a continuous optimization framework for automatic 3D surface shape recovery from noisy image measurements.

In short, the nonlinear FEM models are more accurate but very complex and, in the end, only adapted to very specific applications. One recurring problem is their very high dimensionality, which makes fitting to noisy data problematic. Modal analysis has emerged as one potential solution to this problem. Given a surface represented by an N_v-vertex triangulated mesh, it reduces the number of degrees of freedom by coupling the motion of the vertices into deformation modes obtained by solving the generalized eigenproblem

$$\mathbf{K}\phi = \omega^2 \mathbf{M}\phi \; , \tag{2.2}$$

where $\mathbf{K}$ and $\mathbf{M}$ are the stiffness and mass matrices of Eq. 2.1. The individual ϕ_i and ω_i are the modes and their corresponding frequencies. The displacement of the mesh vertices can then be written as

$$\mathbf{u} = \sum_{i=1}^{3N_v} w_i \phi_i \; , \tag{2.3}$$

where w_i is the amplitude assigned to mode i. The values w_i therefore parameterize the deformation. In theory, there are $3N_v$ modes and thus parameters. In practice, the lower-frequency modes have far more influence on the global surface shape than the higher-frequency ones. It is therefore a valid approximation to discard the latter and to retain only a comparatively small number of the former. Fitting a surface parameterized in this way to image data thus becomes a much lower-dimensional problem. Initially introduced in the field of Computer Vision for image segmentation purposes Pentland and Sclaroff [1991], Pentland [1990], modal analysis was also successfully applied to medical imaging Nastar and Ayache [1996], and non-rigid motion tracking Tao and Huang [1998].

While computationally efficient, modal analysis, as usually applied in our field, assumes a constant stiffness matrix, which implies geometrically and materially linear deformations. This unfortunately never is the case, since it is only true for barely visible deformations. Such models are therefore only rough approximations of the true nonlinear behavior.

2.2 LEARNED DEFORMATION MODELS

The physics-based approach is very attractive because it aims at modeling the true behavior of an object. However, as discussed above, it is very difficult to come up with accurate models. This is both because key physical parameters are often unknown and because there are pervasive nonlinear effects that are very complicated to handle. Doing so would involve computationally expensive algorithms that can get trapped into undesirable local minima. Furthermore, given the usual noisiness of image data, it is not even entirely clear that this expense would truly result in improved accuracy.

As a result, learning models from training data was proposed as an alternative. Rather than trying to guess unknown physical parameters, shape statistics are inferred from available examples and used to instantiate the models. In the following, we briefly introduce the statistical learning methods that have been applied to non-rigid shape recovery.

2.2.1   STATISTICAL LEARNING METHODS

Many surface parameterizations involve a large number of degrees of freedom. This, for example, is the case when specifying the shape of a triangulated mesh in terms of its vertex coordinates. However, these degrees of freedom are often coupled and therefore lie on a much lower-dimensional manifold. Rather than explicitly adding constraints to the problem at hand, the core idea behind statistical learning is to discover this manifold and express the problem in terms of its low-dimensional representation, thus implicitly enforcing the constraints. The different methods are divided into linear and nonlinear ones.

In the linear dimensionality reduction case, an example $\mathbf{x}$ is linked to its latent, possibly low-dimensional, representation $\mathbf{c}$ through the linear relationship

$$\mathbf{x} = \mathbf{x}_0 + \mathbf{Sc} + \epsilon , \qquad (2.4)$$

where $\mathbf{x}_0$ is the mean data value, ϵ accounts for noise, usually taken as Gaussian distributed, and the matrix $\mathbf{S}$ contains the new basis vectors. Typically, $\mathbf{S}$ is obtained by Principal Component Analysis (PCA) Jolliffe [1986]. More specifically, the columns of $\mathbf{S}$ are taken to be the eigenvectors of the data covariance matrix. For non-rigid surfaces, this naturally sorts the deformations from low to high frequencies, as was the case with modal analysis. In fact, when applied to surfaces for which stiffness matrices are also available and modal decomposition can be performed, the resulting deformation modes often look very similar. A probabilistic interpretation of PCA was introduced Tipping and Bishop [1999] and used to build the distribution of the data in the new space from the eigenvalues of the data covariance matrix. To obtain the basis $\mathbf{S}$, PCA can also be replaced by Independent Component Analysis (ICA) Comon [1994]. Instead of yielding uncorrelated components, the basis found by ICA minimizes the dependencies between its potentially non-orthonormal components.

In many cases, however, the low-dimensional manifold onto which the training examples lie is not linear. Therefore, a linear model gives high probabilty to truly unlikely data, or vice-versa. As a result, several nonlinear dimensionality reduction techniques, such as Kernel PCA Schoelkopf et al. [1999], Isomap Tenenbaum et al. [2000], Locally Linear Embedding Roweis and Saul [2000], Laplacian Eigenmaps Belkin and Niyogi [2001], and Maximum Variance Unfolding Weinberger and Saul [2004] were introduced. However, these techniques are not very well-suited to the problem of non-rigid reconstruction, since they do provide a mapping from the low-dimensional representation to the high-dimensional one. Such a mapping must be learned separately, in terms of Radial Basis Functions (RBF) for example, which makes these nonlinear techniques prone to errors both in the direct and the inverse mappings.

As an alternative, one can use the Gaussian Process Latent Variable Model (GPLVM) Lawrence [2004], which was originally introduced as a generalization of probabilistic PCA. The advantage of the GPLVM over the previous nonlinear techniques is that it directly defines a mapping from the low-dimensional representation to the high-dimensional one. This mapping can be written as

$$\mathbf{x} = \sum_i w_i f_i(\mathbf{c}) + \epsilon \,, \tag{2.5}$$

where w_i are the weights of the possibly nonlinear functions f_i of the low-dimensional representation of the manifold $\mathbf{c}$. By placing a simple Gaussian prior on the weights w_i, they can be marginalized out. This yields a multivariate Gaussian conditional density for the data, which can be written as

$$p(\mathbf{X} \mid \mathbf{C}, \Theta) = \frac{1}{\sqrt{(2\pi)^{ND}|\mathbf{K}|^D}} \exp\left(-\frac{1}{2}\mathrm{tr}\left(\mathbf{K}^{-1}\mathbf{X}\mathbf{X}^T\right)\right) \,, \tag{2.6}$$

where $\mathbf{X}$ and $\mathbf{C}$ are the matrices containing the N D-dimensional training examples and their latent representations respectively. $\mathbf{K}$ is a positive-definite covariance matrix whose elements are obtained by evaluating a kernel function k, such that $\mathbf{K}_{i,j} = k(\mathbf{c}_i, \mathbf{c}_j)$. This kernel function is entirely defined by its hyper-parameters Θ, which are optimized at training together with the latent variables $\mathbf{C}$, so as to maximize $p(\mathbf{X} \mid \mathbf{C}, \Theta) p(\mathbf{C}) p(\Theta)$. At inference, the predictive distribution $p(\mathbf{x}_* \mid \mathbf{c}_*, \mathbf{C}, \mathbf{X})$ of a new deformation $\mathbf{x}_*$ given its latent representation $\mathbf{c}_*$ is a Gaussian with mean and variance

$$\mu(\mathbf{c}_*) = \mathbf{X}^T \mathbf{K}^{-1} \mathbf{k}_* \tag{2.7}$$
$$\sigma(\mathbf{c}_*) = k(\mathbf{c}_*, \mathbf{c}_*) - \mathbf{k}_*^T \mathbf{K}^{-1} \mathbf{k}_* \,, \tag{2.8}$$

where $\mathbf{k}_* \in \Re^{N \times 1}$ is the vector containing the covariance function evaluated between the training and the test data. This has the advantage of modeling the uncertainty on the output space to account for the high or low density of training examples in different regions of the space. As a consequence, it allows to build a prior for the shape and its latent representation.

Several extensions of the original GPLVM have been proposed. For instance, to extend the GPLVM to motion data, the Gaussian Process Dynamical Model (GPDM) Wang *et al.* [2005] was introduced. The GPDM allows to model nonlinear relationships between the latent variables corresponding to consecutive frames in a sequence. In a different context, to overcome the burden of evaluating the kernel function between each training latent variable, and thus of having a computation time cubic in N, sparse representations were proposed Lawrence [2007]. In this sparse GPLVM, the kernel is defined in terms of a much smaller number of inducing variables. This makes the GPLVM practical for problems involving many degrees of freedom, therefore requiring large training sets, as is the case of deformable surfaces.

2.2.2 LEARNED MODELS FOR NON-RIGID MODELING

In Computer Vision, the linear learning techniques quickly became very popular. The original Active Shape Models Cootes and Taylor [1992] were extended to full 2D Active Appearance Models (AAM) Cootes *et al.* [1998], Matthews and Baker [2004] to track 2D face deformations. In this case, the model is separated into shape and texture components, both modeled as linear combinations of basis vectors. Adaptations of this were also proposed to group appearance and shape in

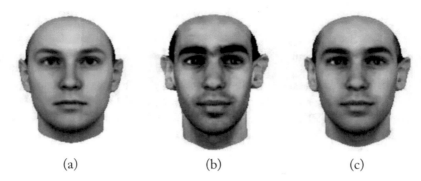

(a)   (b)   (c)

Figure 2.1: Morphable face models Blanz and Vetter [1999]. (a) The average face. (b) Weighted of sum of deformation modes that depicts the face of a specific person. (c) Setting the weights to half the values used in (b) produces an intermediate face. Courtesy of T. Vetter.

a single vector and to mix physics-based approaches with statistical learning Nastar *et al.* [1996]. To account for illumination variations, an Active Illumination and Appearance model was introduced Kahraman *et al.* [2007]. In a similar spirit of being robust to illumination changes, a light-invariant AAM was proposed Pizarro *et al.* [2008], which relies on a light-invariant transformation Finlayson *et al.* [2006]. Finally, hierarchical AAM were introduced to make image fitting more robust and efficient Cosker *et al.* [2004], Peyras *et al.* [2007]. To this end, the fitting process is done in a coarse-to-fine manner, starting from the whole face and refining individual parts.

The AAM were later turned into a Morphable Model Blanz and Vetter [1999], Romdhani and Vetter [2003] designed to recover the full 3D shape of a face, which produced extremely impressive results using a single properly-lit high resolution image. It was also used to model various expressions of a same face Blanz *et al.* [2003] and combined to an AAM to further account for appearance of the face instead of shape only Xiao *et al.* [2004a]. Fig. 2.1 depicts the model and illustrates the fact that the space of faces modeled in this way can indeed be considered as linear since a weighted sum of such models still looks like a face. Because the shape and texture recovery may be perturbed by large cast shadows or specularities, it was later shown that the sensitivity to illumination could be reduced by replacing the appearance-based component of the model by information provided by 2D point correspondences in all pairs of consecutive images of a video sequence in which the head moves rigidly Dimitrijević *et al.* [2004], as shown in Fig. 2.2. This is because such correspondences tend to be affected comparatively little by illumination changes given proper normalization.

Nonlinear methods have also proved useful for Computer Vision applications. In particular, the GPLVM was used to learn a prior on human pose and proved able to generalize well from a small number of training examples Urtasun *et al.* [2005]. Similarly, the GPDM was also applied to constrain the 3D estimation of humans poses in video sequences Urtasun *et al.* [2006]. For non-rigid surface reconstruction, a sparse GPLVM was employed to learn a prior over the deformations of

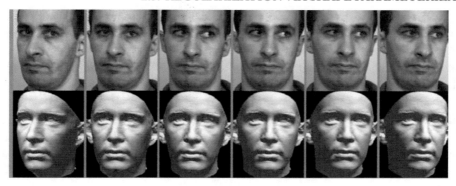

Figure 2.2: Fitting a morphable face model to a low-resolution video sequence. © 2004 IEEE.

local surface patches Salzmann *et al.* [2008b]. The resulting local models have the advantage over the global ones that they can be trained from smaller training sets because local deformations are more constrained than those of a global surface. Furthermore, surface patches can be assembled into arbitrarily shaped global surface meshes, whose 3D deformations can then be recovered without any additional training. This cures one weakness of global models that have to be relearned for each individual surface, even when they all are made of a material seen previously.

    While nonlinear learned models have proved effective to reconstruct complex deformations, they can only be fitted by an iterative scheme that requires an accurate initial estimate. This is due to the non-convexity of the objective functions they yield. As a consequence, they are best suited to tracking application where the initial estimate is provided by the shape computed in the previous frame.

2.3   REGULARIZATION VIA SHAPE PARAMETERIZATION

Learned models have proved very effective for many applications. They remove the need to esti-mate unknown and hard to measure material parameters, while yielding accurate representations of surface deformations. However, some issues remain unsolved. First, gathering enough examples to build a meaningful database represents a very significant amount of work, especially in the case of highly deformable surfaces with many degrees of freedom. Second, registering the examples typically involves a painstaking process. For example, in the case of faces Blanz and Vetter [1999], laser scans first had to be aligned and then remeshed in order to have the same topology. This is why many other models and parameterizations besides physics-based and statistical-learning based ones have also been proposed. Again, several of these approaches were first introduced in the Computer Graphics field for simulation purposes, and were later adapted to recover surface deformations from images.

    Modeling a deformable surface as a triangulated mesh typically yields many degrees of free-dom. However, as mentioned earlier, many of these degrees of freedom are coupled, which can be enforced by using physics-based constraints or by representing the deformations as a combination of basis shapes. An alternative solution to modeling this coupling is to represent the motion of all mesh vertices as a function of a much smaller number of control points. The fine mesh is then obtained by interpolating the deformation between these control points.

One way to achieve this is through the use of Free-Form Deformations. Originally introduced for animation purposes Sederberg and Parry [1986], they were quickly adapted to recover shapes from images Delingette et al. [1991]. Interpolation can be done through Bézier volumes Coquillart [1990], polynomial curves Welch and Witkin [1994], or B-splines Eck and Hoppe [1996], Faloutsos et al. [1997], Krishnamurthy and Levoy [1996]. A disadvantage of standard free-form deformations is their lack of ability to model local deformations. This was overcome by introducing Dirichlet Free-Form Deformations, first to animate a hand Moccozet and Magnenat-Thalmann [1997], and then for model-fitting purposes Ilić and Fua [2002, 2006]. Similarly, RBFs have shown good ability at modeling local deformations when fitting a surface to 3D data Carr et al. [2001]. In that case, the control points act as the centers of the RBFs. A drawback, however, of the control points based techniques is that there is no automated way to create the appropriate set of control points.

An alternative to explicitly relying on control points that define the surface shape is to introduce a multi-resolution approach Hoppe et al. [1994]. In this case, the deformation of an initial coarse mesh is computed, and, following a subdivision strategy Catmull and Clark [1978], Doo and Sabin [1978], the mesh and its deformations are then refined. Several subdivision schemes have been proposed Dyn et al. [1990], Kobbelt [2000], Loop [1987]. Such multi-resolution approaches were also used with dynamic vertex connectivity Kobbelt et al. [2000], and for mesh editing Zorin et al. [1997]. In the latter, a limitation arose from the fact that the editable regions were defined only in the initial coarse mesh. Laplacian surfaces Sorkine et al. [2004], Zhou et al. [2005] were thus proposed to overcome this problem. However, to the best of our knowledge, multi-resolution methods have not been applied in the context of image-based shape recovery. A potential reason might be that the surface is interpolated, which tends to yield visually pleasing results but may not correspond to what is observed in the images.

2.4   LEGACY OF THE PREVIOUS APPROACHES

In the remainder of this survey, we will focus on approaches that tend to be more recent than those discussed above and do not belong to any of the three categories introduced in the previous sections of this chapter. Nevertheless, these newer methods build on some of the components of the earlier ones.

In particular, many methods described below rely on linear subspace models to regularize the shape of the reconstructed surface. For example, in Chapter 4, we will study the use of global and local learned linear models to constrain shape reconstruction from monocular images. In Chapters 5 and 6, we will show that linear global models have also been extensively applied in the context of non-rigid structure-from-motion. In this case, the modes are directly estimated from the 2D tracks of points throughout a video sequence instead of being learned from training data. Representing the deformations of a surface as a linear combination of modes not only bears strong connections to statistical learning techniques, but also to physics-based models and modal analysis.

Even though using linear subspace models effectively reduces the number of degrees of freedom of the problem, monocular reconstruction remains ill-posed and involves many ambiguities. Competing methods can therefore be distinguished by how they go about finding the "best" solution in the space of all possible ones. As we will see, among other things, it can be the one that yields the smoothest surface, that is most temporally consistent, or that best preserves geodesic distances on the surface. Although in general not physically exact, the constraints used for reconstruction are typically inspired by the observed physics of the object of interest.

In Chapter 4, we will also discuss alternative parameterizations that implicitly regularize a surface shape. Specifically, we will present a method that relies on free-form deformations to reconstruct inextensible surfaces. Furthermore, we will discuss approaches designed to model the deformations of developable surfaces, whose shape can be parameterized with very few degrees of freedoms.

Finally, as mentioned in the previous sections for nonlinear FEM and learning techniques, there often is a tradeoff between the accuracy of the model and its practicality. To overcome this weakness, several methods among those described below have introduced regularizers that are both realistic and easy to optimize. For instance, convex formulations were proposed for template-based approaches, as well as closed-form solutions to non-rigid structure-from-motion. While these techniques do not always give the best solutions, they yield a good initial estimate for non-convex, but more accurate formulations of the problem.

CHAPTER 3

Formalizing Template-Based Reconstruction

In this chapter, we focus on template-based approaches to monocular 3D reconstruction and introduce the general formulation of this problem that is common to most such methods. To this end, we rely on a triangulated surface representation and two different kinds of camera models, which we introduce first. We then discuss the 3D-to-2D correspondences that serve as input and derive a linear problem formulation. It is undersconstrained, but forms the basis of many of the techniques of Chapter 4 that impose different kinds of constraints to resolve the ambiguities.

3.1 PROBLEM DEFINITION

Template-based non-rigid 3D reconstruction can be defined as the problem of inferring the 3D shape of a surface in an *input* image, given a *reference* image in which the 3D surface shape is known. Although other surface parameterizations are possible, triangulated meshes are the most common in these kinds of approaches. We will therefore assume that the 3D shape is represented as a triangulated mesh with N_v vertices and N_t facets. The goal then is to recover the 3D vertex locations such that the shape best corresponds to what is observed in the input image.

3.1.1 MOTIVATION

To derive the formulation below, we assume that we can establish correspondences such as those depicted by Fig. 3.1 between the reference and input images. Two main reasons motivated this choice:

- Establishing correspondences between two images does not involve strong assumptions, apart from requiring the surface to be textured. Furthermore, given a reference image, correspondences can be established using either a single input image or a whole video sequence, which means we do not have to track points from image to image, but can if we want to. Consequently, the insights presented here can be used to understand the behavior both of algorithms that rely on correspondences between model and input images, such as those discussed in Chapter 4, and of structure-from-motion algorithms, such as those introduced in Chapter 5 and Chapter 6.

- As shown in Salzmann *et al.* [2007b], relying on image correspondences makes it possible to formalize the shape recovery problem as one of solving an ill-conditioned linear system and

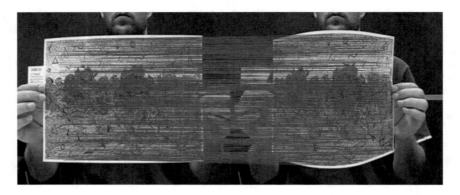

Figure 3.1: Correspondences between a reference image and an input image. The point-to-point correspondences are shown as red lines going from the first image to the second one.

to explicitly exhibit its underlying ambiguities. More specifically, in the *weak perspective* case, which will be defined below, a third of the degrees of freedom is unconstrained. By contrast, in the *full perspective* case, there theoretically is only a scale ambiguity. However, for most realistic scenarios, the same number of degrees of freedom as before are so poorly constrained as to be unconstrained for all practical purposes.

Shape-from-shading techniques Horn and Brooks [1989] offer an alternative to shape-from-correspondences for monocular shape recovery. However, despite many generalizations of the original formulation to account for more realistic shading effects, such as interreflections Forsyth and Zisserman [1991], Nayar *et al.* [1991], specularities Oren and Nayar [1996], shadows Kriegman and Belhumeur [1998], or non-lambertian materials Ahmed and Farag [2006], the resulting solutions are only valid in specific environments. As a consequence, we will only discuss techniques that rely on shading in conjunction with texture.

3.1.2   CAMERA MODELS

In the following analysis, we will assume the internal camera parameters to be known and, as indicated above, we will distinguish between the behavior under the weak and full perspective camera models. We therefore define them below.

Under the weak perspective model, the projection of a 3D point $\mathbf{q}_i$ can be written as

$$d \left[\begin{array}{c} u_i \\ v_i \end{array} \right] = \mathbf{A}' \left(\mathbf{R} \mathbf{q}_i + \mathbf{t} \right) , \tag{3.1}$$

where $\mathbf{A}'$ is the 2×2 matrix of camera internal parameters, $\mathbf{R}$ contains the first two rows of the full camera rotation matrix, $\mathbf{t}$ is the 2×1 camera translation vector, and d is a scalar. In general, d is the same for all the considered 3D points. In the case of the projection of a mesh, we can define a more accurate version of this model by assuming a different affine transform, and thus a different d, for each facet of the mesh. This approximation neglects depth variation across individual facets, rather than across the whole surface. Under this assumption, the projection of a 3D point $\mathbf{q}_i$ lying on facet f of the mesh can be expressed as

$$d_f \begin{bmatrix} u_i \\ v_i \end{bmatrix} = \mathbf{A}' \left(\begin{bmatrix} \mathbf{I}_{2\times2} & | & \mathbf{0} \end{bmatrix} \mathbf{q}_i + \mathbf{0} \right) , \qquad (3.2)$$

where d_f accounts for the average depth of facet f. Here, without loss of generality, we expressed the 3D point in the camera referential, and therefore replaced $\mathbf{R}$ with the first two rows of the 3×3 identity matrix and the translation with a zero vector. Note that this does not prevent us from accounting for camera motion. It simply means that it will be interpreted as a rigid motion of the object of interest.

Under the full perspective model, the projection of a 3D point $\mathbf{q}_i$ is written as

$$d_i \begin{bmatrix} u_i \\ v_i \\ 1 \end{bmatrix} = \mathbf{A} \left(\mathbf{I}_{3\times3}\mathbf{q}_i + \mathbf{0} \right) , \qquad (3.3)$$

where the matrix of internal camera parameters $\mathbf{A}$ is now a 3×3 matrix, and each point i has a different depth factor d_i.

3.2   3D-TO-2D CORRESPONDENCES

Detecting feature points in images has received enormous attention in the Computer Vision community. For most template-based approaches, feature points are typically detected with either the SIFT keypoints detector Lowe [2004] or Harris's corners detector Harris and Stephens [1988]. Once feature points have been detected in two images, they need to be matched to produce correspondences. When using SIFT, this can be done by a simple dot-product between specific vector representations of the feature points. For Harris's corners, methods based on Randomized Trees have proved efficient Lepetit and Fua [2006]. From a large set of views obtained by applying random affine transformations to a reference image, a tree that models the relationships between neighboring keypoints is built. Each leaf-node of the tree then corresponds to a specific keypoint, and matching can be done by dropping the feature points of a new image down the tree.

Another way to establish correspondences is to first tackle the 2D non-rigid image registration problem. Non-rigid image registration aims at finding a transformation between two images of the same surface undergoing different deformations. Different parameterizations have been proposed to represent the transformation, such as RBFs Bartoli and Zisserman [2004], thin-plate splines Bookstein [1989], or 2D meshes Pilet et al. [2008]. Since the resulting warp is defined over the entire image, discrete correespondences can then be obtained by sampling it. Note that, while 2D non-rigid registration can be thought of as related to 3D non-rigid reconstruction, we believe

Figure 3.2: Obtaining image correspondences. A feature point is detected in the reference image, shown in the middle. Knowing the reference 3D shape of the mesh, on the left, and the camera projection matrix, we can retrieve the facet to which the feature point belongs, and define the point in terms of its barycentric coordinates. The feature point can then be matched against points detected in the input image, shown on the right. This yields 3D-to-2D correspondences in terms of the unknown 3D mesh vertices in the input image.

that methods addressing the 2D case deserve their own separate review. Therefore, we will limit the study in this survey to 3D reconstruction techniques.

For template-based approaches, the matches are established between the current image of interest and the reference image, in which the 3D shape and the camera calibration are known, as depicted in Fig. 3.2. Under such assumptions, the 3D locations of the feature points on the template can be computed by intersecting the ray between the camera center and the 2D image measurement with the facets of the triangulated mesh. This lets us represent a 3D point in terms of its barycentric coordinates with respect to the vertices of the facet intersected by the ray. This yields 3D-to-2D correspondences for the current image, where the 3D positions of the feature points are defined with respect to the unknown 3D positions of the mesh vertices. To recover the 3D shape, the idea is then to find the position of the mesh vertices that minimizes the distance between the detected 2D features and the 3D points locations projected into the image.

3.3   LINEAR FORMULATION

In this section, we show that recovering the 3D shape of a non-rigid surface from 3D-to-2D correspondences such as those introduced in Section 3.2 amounts to solving a linear system. Under the weak perspective projection model, exactly one third of the singular values of the corresponding matrix are zero, which accounts for depth ambiguities. Under the full perspective model, only one is strictly zero but the same one third are so small as to make the system extremely ill-conditioned.

3.3.1   AMBIGUITIES UNDER WEAK PERSPECTIVE PROJECTION

We now show how computing the 3D mesh vertex coordinates given 3D-to-2D correspondences in the weak perspective case can be formulated as the solution to a linear system and discuss its degeneracies. We start with a mesh containing a single triangle and extend our result to a complete one.

3.3.1.1 Projection of a 3D Surface Point

Recall from Eq. 3.2 that under a weak perspective model, the projection to a 2D image plane of a 3D point $\mathbf{q}_i$ whose coordinates are expressed in the camera referential can be written as

$$d \begin{bmatrix} u_i \\ v_i \end{bmatrix} = \mathbf{P}'\mathbf{q}_i , \quad \mathbf{P}' = \mathbf{A}' \begin{bmatrix} \mathbf{I}_{2\times 2} & | & \mathbf{0} \end{bmatrix} \tag{3.4}$$

where d is a depth factor associated to the weak perspective camera and $\mathbf{A}'$ is a 2×2 matrix representing the camera internal parameters.

If $\mathbf{q}_i$ lies on the facet of a triangulated mesh, it can be expressed as a weighted sum of the facet vertices. Eq. 3.4 becomes

$$d \begin{bmatrix} u_i \\ v_i \end{bmatrix} = \mathbf{P}'(a_i\mathbf{v}_1 + b_i\mathbf{v}_2 + c_i\mathbf{v}_3) , \tag{3.5}$$

where $\mathbf{v}_i {}_{,1\leq i\leq 3}$ are the vectors of 3D vertex coordinates and (a_i, b_i, c_i) the barycentric coordinates of $\mathbf{q}_i$.

3.3.1.2 Reconstructing a Single Facet

Let us assume that we are given a list of N_c^t 3D-to-2D correspondences for points lying inside one single facet. The coordinates of its three vertices $\mathbf{v}_i {}_{,1\leq i\leq 3}$ can be computed by solving the linear system

$$\begin{bmatrix} a_1\mathbf{P}' & b_1\mathbf{P}' & c_1\mathbf{P}' & -\begin{bmatrix} u_1 \\ v_1 \end{bmatrix} \\ \cdots & \cdots & \cdots & \cdots \\ a_i\mathbf{P}' & b_i\mathbf{P}' & c_i\mathbf{P}' & -\begin{bmatrix} u_i \\ v_i \end{bmatrix} \\ \cdots & \cdots & \cdots & \cdots \\ a_{N_c^t}\mathbf{P}' & b_{N_c^t}\mathbf{P}' & c_{N_c^t}\mathbf{P}' & -\begin{bmatrix} u_{N_c^t} \\ v_{N_c^t} \end{bmatrix} \end{bmatrix} \begin{bmatrix} \mathbf{v}_1 \\ \mathbf{v}_2 \\ \mathbf{v}_3 \\ d \end{bmatrix} = \mathbf{0} , \tag{3.6}$$

where d is treated as an auxiliary variable to recover as well. Since we only have one facet, we also only have one projection matrix. Thus, only a single d corresponding to the average depth of the facet is necessary and all $[u_i, v_i]^T$ can be put in the same column.

Since $\mathbf{P}'$ is of size 2×3, it has at most rank 2. Moreover, we can show that the last column of the global matrix also is a linear combination of the two first columns of $\mathbf{P}'$ by writing

$$
\begin{aligned}
\begin{bmatrix} u_i \\ v_i \end{bmatrix} &= \mathbf{P}'\frac{1}{d}(a_i\mathbf{v}_1 + b_i\mathbf{v}_2 + c_i\mathbf{v}_3) \\
&= \begin{bmatrix} \mathbf{A}' \mid \mathbf{0} \end{bmatrix}\frac{1}{d}(a_i\mathbf{v}_1 + b_i\mathbf{v}_2 + c_i\mathbf{v}_3) \\
&= \frac{a_i}{d}\mathbf{A}'\begin{bmatrix} \mathbf{v}_{1,1} \\ \mathbf{v}_{1,2} \end{bmatrix} + \frac{b_i}{d}\mathbf{A}'\begin{bmatrix} \mathbf{v}_{2,1} \\ \mathbf{v}_{2,2} \end{bmatrix} + \frac{c_i}{d}\mathbf{A}'\begin{bmatrix} \mathbf{v}_{3,1} \\ \mathbf{v}_{3,2} \end{bmatrix},
\end{aligned}
\tag{3.7}
$$

where $\mathbf{v}_{i,j}$ is the jth coordinate of vertex $\mathbf{v}_i$. The coefficients of Eq. 3.7 are independent of the correspondence considered and are therefore valid for any row i of the matrix. This means that the entire last column can be expressed as a linear combination of the other columns of the matrix. Thus, when $N_c^t \geq 3$, the rank of the matrix of Eq. 3.6 is always 6.

3.3.1.3 Reconstructing the Whole Mesh

As discussed above, when there are several triangles, using the weak perspective model amounts to introducing a projection matrix per facet. However, since in reality we only have one camera, its internal parameters, rotation matrix, and center are bound to be the same for each triangle. This only lets us with a variable depth factor d_f for each facet f among the N_t facets of the mesh. We can then write the system

$$
\mathbf{M}'_{\mathbf{m}}\begin{bmatrix} \mathbf{v}_1 \\ \dots \\ \mathbf{v}_{N_v} \\ d_1 \\ \dots \\ d_{N_t} \end{bmatrix} = \mathbf{0},
\tag{3.8}
$$

with

$$
\mathbf{M}'_{\mathbf{m}} = \begin{bmatrix}
a_1\mathbf{P}' & b_1\mathbf{P}' & c_1\mathbf{P}' & 0 & \dots & \dots & -\begin{bmatrix} u_1 \\ v_1 \end{bmatrix} & 0 & \dots & \dots & \dots \\
\dots & \dots & \dots & \dots & \dots & \dots & \dots & \dots & \dots & \dots & \dots \\
0 & b_j\mathbf{P}' & c_j\mathbf{P}' & d_j\mathbf{P}' & 0 & \dots & 0 & -\begin{bmatrix} u_j \\ v_j \end{bmatrix} & 0 & \dots & \dots \\
\dots & \dots & \dots & \dots & \dots & \dots & \dots & \dots & \dots & \dots & \dots \\
a_l\mathbf{P}' & 0 & c_l\mathbf{P}' & 0 & e_l\mathbf{P}' & \dots & 0 & \dots & -\begin{bmatrix} u_l \\ v_l \end{bmatrix} & 0 & \dots \\
\dots & \dots & \dots & \dots & \dots & \dots & \dots & \dots & \dots & \dots & \dots
\end{bmatrix}.
$$

The left half of $\mathbf{M}'_{\mathbf{m}}$, which is of size $2N_c \times 3N_v$, N_c being the total number of correspondences, has at most rank $2N_v$ because $\mathbf{P}'$ has rank 2. We can then show that its right half, which is of size $2N_c \times N_t$, has at most rank $N_t - 1$. To this end, we need to show that its last column can be expressed as a linear combination of the others. Assuming point N_c belongs to facet f, we can write

$$- \begin{bmatrix} u_{N_c} \\ v_{N_c} \end{bmatrix} = -\frac{a_{N_c}}{d_f} \mathbf{A}' \begin{bmatrix} \mathbf{v}_{f,1,1} \\ \mathbf{v}_{f,1,2} \end{bmatrix} - \frac{b_{N_c}}{d_f} \mathbf{A}' \begin{bmatrix} \mathbf{v}_{f,2,1} \\ \mathbf{v}_{f,2,2} \end{bmatrix} - \frac{c_{N_c}}{d_f} \mathbf{A}' \begin{bmatrix} \mathbf{v}_{f,3,1} \\ \mathbf{v}_{f,3,2} \end{bmatrix} , \qquad (3.9)$$

where $\mathbf{v}_{f,i,j}$ is the jth coordinate of the ith vertex of facet f. This shows that the bottom two rows of the last column can be written as a linear function of the other columns. However, computing this linear combination would introduce non-zero terms on the higher rows of the last column. For points also belonging to facet f, these terms are directly canceled, as suggested by Eq. 3.7. For points belonging to facets sharing no vertices with facet f, these values will be zero. For point i belonging to a facet l sharing two vertices with facet f, the value will be

$$-\frac{a_i}{d_f} \mathbf{A}' \begin{bmatrix} \mathbf{v}_{f,1,1} \\ \mathbf{v}_{f,1,2} \end{bmatrix} - \frac{b_i}{d_f} \mathbf{A}' \begin{bmatrix} \mathbf{v}_{f,2,1} \\ \mathbf{v}_{f,2,2} \end{bmatrix} = \frac{d_l}{d_f} \left(- \begin{bmatrix} u_i \\ v_i \end{bmatrix} + \frac{c_i}{d_l} \mathbf{A}' \begin{bmatrix} \mathbf{v}_{l,3,1} \\ \mathbf{v}_{l,3,2} \end{bmatrix} \right) . \qquad (3.10)$$

Therefore, this value also is a linear combination of the other columns of $\mathbf{M}'_\mathbf{m}$. Similar reasoning can be done for facets sharing a single vertex with f. As a consequence, all terms introduced on the last column by using the linear combination of Eq. 3.9 can be canceled, which means that this last column is a linear combination of the others, and thus that the right half of $\mathbf{M}'_\mathbf{m}$ has at most rank $N_t - 1$. This means that for a full mesh, $\mathbf{M}'_\mathbf{m}$ has at most rank $2N_v + N_t - 1$. This leaves us with $N_v + 1$ ambiguities. This seems natural due first to the scale ambiguity and second to the fact that each vertex is free to move along its line of sight without affecting the reprojection of points inside the facets.

3.3.2   AMBIGUITIES UNDER FULL PERSPECTIVE PROJECTION

As in the weak perspective case, we show that, given 3D-to-2D correspondences, the coordinates of the mesh vertices must be solution to a linear system by starting with a mesh containing a single triangle and extending our result to a complete mesh.

3.3.2.1   Projection of a 3D Surface Point
Recall from Eq. 3.3 that the perspective projection of a 3D point $\mathbf{q}_i$ expressed in camera coordinates can be written as

$$d_i \begin{bmatrix} u_i \\ v_i \\ 1 \end{bmatrix} = \mathbf{A}\mathbf{q}_i , \qquad (3.11)$$

where $\mathbf{A}$ is the internal parameters matrix, and d_i a scalar accounting for depth.

As before, if $\mathbf{q}_i$ lies on the facet of a triangulated mesh, it can be expressed as a weighted sum of the facet vertices. Eq. 3.11 then becomes

$$d_i \begin{bmatrix} u_i \\ v_i \\ 1 \end{bmatrix} = \mathbf{A}(a_i\mathbf{v}_1 + b_i\mathbf{v}_2 + c_i\mathbf{v}_3) , \qquad (3.12)$$

where $\mathbf{v}_i$ $_{,1\leq i \leq 3}$ are the vectors of 3D vertices coordinates and (a_i, b_i, c_i) the barycentric coordinates of $\mathbf{q}_i$.

3.3.2.2   Reconstructing a Single Facet

Given the same N_c^t 3D-to-2D correspondences lying inside one single facet as in the weak perspective case, its vertex coordinates $\mathbf{v}_i$ $_{,1\leq i \leq 3}$ can be computed by solving the following equation where the d_i are treated as auxiliary variables to be recovered as well

$$
\mathbf{M_f}
\begin{bmatrix}
\mathbf{v}_1 \\
\mathbf{v}_2 \\
\mathbf{v}_3 \\
d_1 \\
\dots \\
d_i \\
\dots \\
d_{N_c^t}
\end{bmatrix}
= \mathbf{0} ,
\tag{3.13}
$$

with

$$
\mathbf{M_f} =
\begin{bmatrix}
a_1\mathbf{A} & b_1\mathbf{A} & c_1\mathbf{A} & -\begin{bmatrix} u_1 \\ v_1 \\ 1 \end{bmatrix} & 0 & \dots & \dots & \dots \\
\dots & \dots & \dots & \dots & \dots & \dots & \dots & \dots \\
a_i\mathbf{A} & b_i\mathbf{A} & c_i\mathbf{A} & 0 & \dots & -\begin{bmatrix} u_i \\ v_i \\ 1 \end{bmatrix} & 0 & \dots \\
\dots & \dots & \dots & \dots & \dots & \dots & \dots & \dots \\
a_{N_c^t}\mathbf{A} & b_{N_c^t}\mathbf{A} & c_{N_c^t}\mathbf{A} & 0 & \dots & \dots & \dots & -\begin{bmatrix} u_{N_c^t} \\ v_{N_c^t} \\ 1 \end{bmatrix}
\end{bmatrix} .
$$

For $N_c^t > 4$, if the columns of $\mathbf{M_f}$ had become linearly independent, the system would then have had a unique solution. However, this is not what happens.

To prove that $\mathbf{M_f}$ is rank-deficient, we show that its last column can always be written as a linear combination of the others as follows. From Eq. 3.12 we can write

$$
-\begin{bmatrix} u_{N_c^t} \\ v_{N_c^t} \\ 1 \end{bmatrix} = a_{N_c^t}\mathbf{A}\lambda_1 + b_{N_c^t}\mathbf{A}\lambda_2 + c_{N_c^t}\mathbf{A}\lambda_3 ,
\tag{3.14}
$$

where $\lambda_j = -\mathbf{v}_j/d_{N_c^t}$ for $1 \leq j \leq 3$. For all $1 \leq i < N_c^t$, we have

$$a_i \mathbf{A}\lambda_1 + b_i \mathbf{A}\lambda_2 + c_i \mathbf{A}\lambda_3 = -\frac{a_i}{d_{N_c^t}}\mathbf{A}\mathbf{v}_1 - \frac{b_i}{d_{N_c^t}}\mathbf{A}\mathbf{v}_2 - \frac{c_i}{d_{N_c^t}}\mathbf{A}\mathbf{v}_3$$

$$= -\frac{d_i}{d_{N_c^t}}\begin{bmatrix} u_i \\ v_i \\ 1 \end{bmatrix}.$$

This implies that the last column of the matrix $\mathbf{M_f}$ of Eq. 3.13 is indeed a linear combination of the previous ones with coefficients $(\lambda_1^T, \lambda_2^T, \lambda_3^T, -d_1/d_{N_c^t}, ..., -d_{N_c^t-1}/d_{N_c^t})$. In the general case, none of these coefficients is zero. Furthermore, because $\mathbf{A}$ has full rank and the barycentric coordinates are independent in general, the first 9 columns of $\mathbf{M_f}$ are linearly independent. Thus, given the particular structure of the right half of $\mathbf{M_f}$, trying to write any column as a linear combination of all the others except the last one would yield wrong values on the last three rows, which could only be corrected by using the last column. This implies that, in general, $\mathbf{M_f}$ has full rank minus 1.

3.3.2.3 Reconstructing the Whole Mesh

If we now consider a mesh made of $N_v > 3$ vertices with a total of N_c correspondences well-spread over the whole mesh, Eq. 3.13 becomes

$$\mathbf{M_m} \begin{bmatrix} \mathbf{v}_1 \\ ... \\ \mathbf{v}_{N_v} \\ d_1 \\ ... \\ d_{N_c} \end{bmatrix} = \mathbf{0}, \tag{3.15}$$

with

$$\mathbf{M_m} = \begin{bmatrix} a_1\mathbf{A} & b_1\mathbf{A} & c_1\mathbf{A} & 0 & ... & ... & -\begin{bmatrix} u_1 \\ v_1 \\ 1 \end{bmatrix} & 0 & ... & ... & ... \\ ... & ... & ... & ... & ... & ... & ... & ... & ... & ... & ... \\ 0 & b_j\mathbf{A} & c_j\mathbf{A} & d_j\mathbf{A} & 0 & ... & 0 & -\begin{bmatrix} u_j \\ v_j \\ 1 \end{bmatrix} & 0 & ... & ... \\ ... & ... & ... & ... & ... & ... & ... & ... & ... & ... & ... \\ a_l\mathbf{A} & 0 & c_l\mathbf{A} & 0 & e_l\mathbf{A} & ... & 0 & ... & -\begin{bmatrix} u_l \\ v_l \\ 1 \end{bmatrix} & 0 & ... \\ ... & ... & ... & ... & ... & ... & ... & ... & ... & ... & ... \end{bmatrix}.$$

Coefficients similar to those of Eq. 3.14 can be derived to compute $\begin{bmatrix} u_{N_c}, v_{N_c}, 1 \end{bmatrix}^T$ as a linear combination of the non-zero columns of the last row. Following a similar reasoning as in the weak perspective case, it can easily be checked that the last column of the matrix can be expressed as a linear combination of the others, which then are linearly independent. Thus, matrix $\mathbf{M_m}$ of Eq. 3.15 has still full rank minus 1. This reflects the well-known scale ambiguity in monocular vision.

Representing the problem as in Eq. 3.15 was convenient to discuss the rank of the matrix. However, in practice, we want to recover the vertex coordinates but are not interested in having the d_i as unknowns. We therefore eliminate them by rewriting Eq. 3.15 as

$$\mathbf{M}\begin{bmatrix} \mathbf{v}_1 \\ ... \\ \mathbf{v}_{N_v} \end{bmatrix} = \mathbf{0} \,, \tag{3.16}$$

with

$$\mathbf{M} = \begin{bmatrix} a_1\mathbf{T_1} & b_1\mathbf{T_1} & c_1\mathbf{T_1} & 0 & ... & ... \\ ... & ... & ... & ... & ... & ... \\ 0 & b_j\mathbf{T_j} & c_j\mathbf{T_j} & d_j\mathbf{T_j} & 0 & ... \\ ... & ... & ... & ... & ... & ... \\ a_l\mathbf{T_1} & 0 & c_l\mathbf{T_1} & 0 & e_l\mathbf{T_1} & ... \\ ... & ... & ... & ... & ... & \end{bmatrix} \,, \text{ and } \mathbf{T_i} = \mathbf{A}_{2\times3} - \begin{bmatrix} u_i\mathbf{A}_3 \\ v_i\mathbf{A}_3 \end{bmatrix} \,,$$

where $\mathbf{A}_3$ represents the last row of matrix $\mathbf{A}$ and $\mathbf{A}_{2\times3}$ its first two rows. Since $\mathbf{M}$ has the same rank as matrix $\mathbf{M_m}$ by construction, the previous and following results are valid for both representations of the problem.

3.3.2.4 Effective Rank

In the previous paragraph, we showed that $\mathbf{M}$ has at most full rank minus one. However, this does not tell the whole story: In general, it is ill-conditioned and many of its singular values are so small that, in practice, it should be treated as a matrix of even lower rank. To illustrate this point, we projected randomly sampled points on the facets of the synthetic 88-vertices mesh of Fig. 3.3 (a) using a known camera model. We then computed the singular values of $\mathbf{M}$, which we plot in Fig. 3.3 (b). Even though only one of these values is exactly zero, we can see that they drop down drastically after the first $2N_v = 176$. This shows that, even though the matrix may have full rank minus 1, the solution of the linear system would be very sensitive to noise. Therefore, in a real situation, we would actually be closer to having N_v ambiguities. In Fig. 3.4, we show the effect of adding two of the corresponding singular vectors—one associated to the zero singular value and the other to a small one—to the mesh in its reference position.

Intuitively, the 3D-to-2D correspondences constrain the mesh vertices to move along lines of sight but their exact distance to the camera is poorly constrained because changing it only results in minor reprojection errors for points lying inside the facets. As a consequence, the number of degrees of freedom corresponds to the one derived for the weak perspective case in Section 3.3.1.3, except

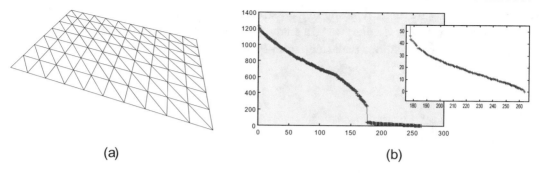

(a) (b)

Figure 3.3: Effective rank of matrix **M**. (a) 88-vertex mesh seen from the viewpoint used for reconstruction. (b) Singular values of **M** for the mesh of (a). Note how the values drop down after the $2N_v = 176^{th}$ one. Although **M** was obtained with a full perspective model, this corresponds to the value predicted by the weak perspective model of Section 3.3.1. The small graph on the right is a magnified version of the part of the graph containing the small singular values. The last one is zero up to the precision of the Matlab routine used to compute it and the others are not very much larger.

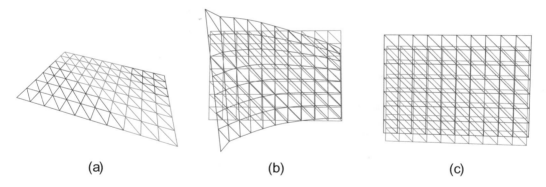

(a) (b) (c)

Figure 3.4: Visualizing vectors associated to small singular values. (a) Reference mesh and mesh to which one the vectors has been added seen from the original viewpoint, in which they are almost indistinguishable. (b) The same two meshes seen from a different viewpoint. (c) The reference mesh modified by adding the vector associated to the zero singular value. Note that the resulting deformation corresponds to a global scaling.

that the global scale is directly related to the position of the vertices along the lines of sight, which produces one fewer small singular value.

The fact that the depth of the mesh vertices is ill-constrained shows that 3D-to-2D correspondences on their own are not sufficient to reconstruct the shape of a surface from a monocular image. Therefore, additional knowledge must be introduced in the problem. This can be done by taking into account other sources of image information, such as shading. However, as mentioned earlier, the resulting methods typically rely on strong assumptions that are only valid for specific cases. Instead, in the next chapter, we will study the introduction of additional shape constraints, and discuss several formulations that range from specific to a particular problem to more generally applicable.

CHAPTER 4

Performing Template-Based Reconstruction

As discussed in Chapter 3, given N_c point correspondences between a reference image in which the 3D shape is known and an input image, recovering the new shape in that image amounts to solving the linear system of Eq. 3.16. We write it here again as

$$\mathbf{Mx} = \mathbf{0} \text{ , where } \mathbf{x} = \begin{bmatrix} \mathbf{v}_1 \\ \dots \\ \mathbf{v}_{N_v} \end{bmatrix} , \tag{4.1}$$

$\mathbf{v}_i$ contains the 3D coordinates of the ith vertex of the N_v-vertex triangulated mesh representing the surface, and $\mathbf{M}$ is a matrix that depends on the coordinates of correspondences in the input image and on the camera internal parameters. A solution of this system defines a surface such that 3D feature points that project at specific locations in the reference image reproject at matching locations in the input image. Solving this system in the least-squares sense therefore yields surfaces for which the overall *reprojection error* is small.

Note, however, that this is not strictly equivalent to minimizing the reprojection error because computing the actual reprojection of a 3D point on the image plane would involve a division by the depth factors d_i of Eq. 3.15, thus yielding nonlinear terms. In essence, solving this linear system is equivalent to performing a Direct Linear Transformation (DLT) Hartley and Zisserman [2000], which gives a different weight to each correspondence according to its distance to the camera and therefore potentially reduces accuracy. Even more problematically, $\mathbf{M}$ is a $2N_c \times 3N_v$ matrix with at least N_v singular values that are very small, as shown in Fig. 3.3. Because the system is so ill-conditioned, many different shapes can produce very similar projections, and even small imprecisions in the point coordinates, and consequently in the coefficients of $\mathbf{M}$, can lead to large reconstruction errors.

In this chapter, we will review some of the approaches that have been proposed to overcome these ambiguities and increase accuracy either by enforcing temporal consistency across images in video sequences, or by enforcing additional geometric constraints, such as smoothness and preservation of geodesic distances across the surface.

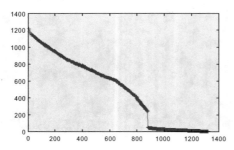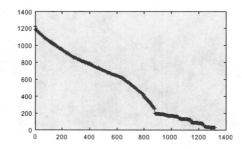

Figure 4.1: Singular values for a 5 frames sequence under perspective projection based on Salzmann *et al.* [2007b]. Left: Without temporal consistency constraints between frames, the linear system is ill-constrained. Right: Bounding the frame-to-frame displacements transforms the ill-conditioned linear system into a well-conditioned one. The smaller singular values have increased and are now clearly non-zero. Since our motion model introduces more equations than strictly necessary, the other values are also affected, but only very slightly.

4.1   IMPOSING TEMPORAL CONSISTENCY

When dealing with video sequences, one can assume that the surface does not move randomly between consecutive frames, whatever its physical properties. One way to overcome the rank deficiency of the matrix of Eq. 4.1 is therefore to perform the reconstruction over several frames simultaneously. This amounts to stacking the coordinate vectors $\mathbf{x}$ of Eq. 4.1, one for each time frame, and creating a block diagonal matrix whose elements are matrices $\mathbf{M}$, again one for each time frame. Without temporal constraints to link the coordinate vectors across frames, this system is just as ill-conditioned as before. However, because displacement speeds are limited, the range of frame-to-frame motion is always bounded, which can be expressed as a set of additional linear constraints of the form

$$\mathbf{x}^t - \mathbf{x}^{t-1} = \mathbf{0} \; , \; 2 \leq t \leq N_f \; , \tag{4.2}$$

where $\mathbf{x}^t$ is the coordinate vector for frame t and N_f is the total number of frames. These constraints link the coordinate vectors and can be added to the correspondence equations in the joint system for all N_f frames. The resulting linear system is much better-conditioned as depicted by Fig. 4.1. Since this system is solved in the least-squares sense, the motion equations will not be truly enforced, and thus some motion will be allowed. As a result, given the shape at the beginning and at the end of a sequence, the surface can be simultaneously reconstructed over the whole sequence as shown in Fig. 4.2.

These simple temporal constraints, however, do not accurately model the true dynamical behavior of a non-rigid surface and, as a result, the reconstructions are not necessarily very accurate. Furthermore, as discussed above, solving the linear system of Eq. 4.1 in the least-squares sense is not strictly equivalent to minimizing the true reprojection error. In Salzmann *et al.* [2007a], this was remedied by exploiting techniques proposed for rigid object modeling Kahl [2005], Ke and Kanade

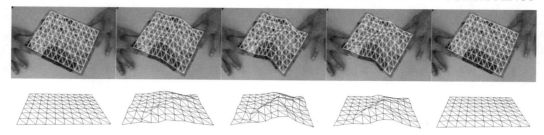

Figure 4.2: Reconstruction results for a very flexible plastic sheet. In spite of the many creases, the overall shape is correctly recovered up to small errors due to erroneous correspondences. © 2007 IEEE.

[2005], Sim and Hartley [2006] that expressed the minimization of the true reprojection error as a Second Order Cone Programming (SOCP) problem Boyd and Vandenberghe [2004]. In its general form, an SOCP can be written as

$$\underset{\mathbf{x}}{\text{minimize}} \quad \mathbf{f}^T\mathbf{x} \tag{4.3}$$
$$\text{subject to} \quad \|\mathbf{A}_i\mathbf{x} + \mathbf{b}_i\|_2 \leq \mathbf{c}_i^T\mathbf{x} + d_i \ , \ 1 \leq i \leq m \ ,$$

where $\mathbf{f}$ is the vector that defines the objective function, $\mathbf{A}_i$ is a matrix, $\mathbf{b}_i$ and $\mathbf{c}_i$ are vectors, and d_i is a scalar. Problems of this type are convex and, thus, have a unique minimum that can be found very effectively using available packages such as SeDuMi Sturm [1999]. Furthermore, SOCP can be used to formulate problems more general than linear programming, quadratic programming and quadratically-constrained quadratic programming.

For the specific case of deformable surface reconstruction, minimizing the reprojection error can be expressed as

$$\underset{\gamma,\mathbf{x}}{\text{minimize}} \quad \gamma \tag{4.4}$$
$$\text{subject to} \quad \left\|\left[(\mathbf{P}_1 - u_i\mathbf{P}_3)\mathbf{h}_i, \ (\mathbf{P}_2 - v_i\mathbf{P}_3)\mathbf{h}_i\right]\right\|_2 \leq \gamma\mathbf{P}_3\tilde{\mathbf{q}}_i \ , \ 1 \leq i \leq N_c \ ,$$

where $\mathbf{P}_k$ contains the kth line of the projection matrix, and $\tilde{\mathbf{q}}_i = \left[\mathbf{q}_i^T, 1\right]^T$ is the vector of homogeneous coordinates of the 3D point matching the ith feature point. $\tilde{\mathbf{q}}_i$ is obtained from the vertex coordinates $\mathbf{x}$ and barycentric coordinates. γ is an additional slack variable that encodes the maximum reprojection error for all feature points.

While a solution of the above problem minimizes the true reprojection error, it still is underconstrained. This is why temporal consistency was introduced in Salzmann *et al.* [2007a], to prevent the orientation of mesh edges from varying excessively from one frame to the next, as illustrated in Fig. 4.3. This can be expressed as additional SOCP constraints of the form

$$\left\|\mathbf{v}_j^{t+1} - \left(\mathbf{v}_i^{t+1} + l_{i,j}\frac{\mathbf{v}_j^t - \mathbf{v}_i^t}{\|\mathbf{v}_j^t - \mathbf{v}_i^t\|_2}\right)\right\|_2 \leq \lambda l_{i,j} \ , \tag{4.5}$$

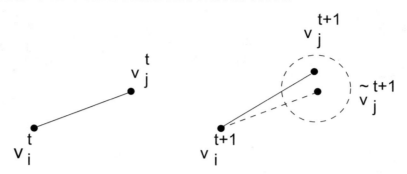

Figure 4.3: The orientation of the edge between $\mathbf{v}_i$ and $\mathbf{v}_j$ at time $t+1$ is predicted to be the same as at time t. The distance between the true vertex $\mathbf{v}_j^{t+1}$ and its prediction $\tilde{\mathbf{v}}_j^{t+1}$ is then constrained to be less than some specified value.

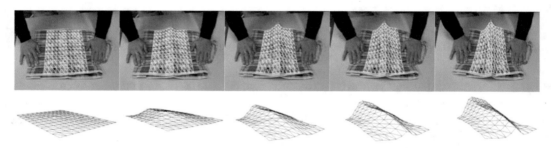

Figure 4.4:   Recovering the deformations of a plastic bag with a sharp crease in it from an 86-frames video using the Salzmann *et al.* [2007a] method. © 2007 IEEE.

where $l_{i,j}$ is the original length of the edge between vertices i and j, and λ encodes the amount of possible motion. These temporal constraints have the advantage of being more realistic than the ones of Eq. 4.2 and can handle highly-deformable surfaces such as the one of Fig. 4.4 without adding unwarranted smoothness. It was later shown that the resulting problem could be reformulated as an unconstrained quadratic optimization problem, which is even easier to solve Zhu *et al.* [2008]. To this end, the SOCP correspondence constraints of the problem in Eq. 4.4 are turned into equalities by introducing one slack variable for each correspondence. The sum of these slack variables can then be expressed as a quadratic function of the shape, and directly minimized in the objective function. The edge orientation constraints are either kept as constraints to yield a QP problem, or re-written as a quadratic regularizer, thus resulting in an unconstrained optimization problem. Fig. 4.5 depicts the reconstruction error of these two formulations, and compares them against the results of the SOCP approach. The reconstruction error is given as the mean vertex-to-vertex distance between ground-truth and the recovered surface.

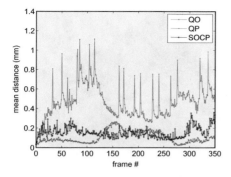 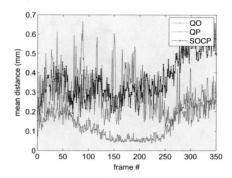

Figure 4.5: Comparison of the accuracies obtained with the SOCP formulation based on Salzmann *et al.* [2007a] with the QP and unconstrained (QO) formulations of Zhu *et al.* [2008]. Reconstructions were obtained with image noise variance 1 (left) and 2 (right). Note that the QP and QO approaches yield better results than the SOCP one. Courtesy of J. Zhu.

4.2 IMPOSING GEOMETRIC CONSTRAINTS

The methods discussed in the previous section are very generic in that they make very few assumptions on the smoothness or physical properties of the surface. However, they are all limited by the fact that they involve frame-to-frame tracking and are therefore subject to drift and irrecoverable failure if there are too few valid correspondences in any given frame. Furthermore, they require a full video sequence, as well as an initial shape estimate for the first frame, either of which may not be available.

A useful alternative is therefore to replace temporal consistency constraints by geometric ones that allow reconstruction using a single input image or a very short sequence of consecutive ones. The difficulty then is to design the constraints so as to make as few unwarranted assumptions on the allowable surface deformations as possible. In the remainder of this section, we classify approaches according to how stringent the constraints are. We start with developable surfaces, whose deformations are very strongly constrained. We then move on to surfaces that deform smoothly, including those that remain globally smooth and those that need only be locally smooth and can therefore develop creases. We conclude by discussing inextensible surfaces.

4.2.1 DEVELOPABLE SURFACES

Developable surfaces are surfaces with zero Gaussian curvature, meaning that, for all points and all possible deformations, one of the principal curvatures must be zero. Such 3D surfaces can be flattened onto a plane without distortion and are ruled surfaces. For example, initially flat pieces of paper are developable and are often used to demonstrate techniques that rely on this property.

As shown in Gumerov *et al.* [2004], given only surface boundaries in both the reference and input image acquired by a calibrated camera, it is possible to recover the 3D structure by solving Ordinary Differential Equations. Another approach is to explicitly parameterize the reference surface

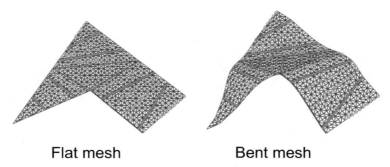

Figure 4.6: In Perriollat and Bartoli [2007], a developable surface is parameterized with a set of guiding rules, drawn in pink, and their corresponding bending angle. Courtesy of A. Bartoli. © 2007 IEEE.

in terms of guiding rules and their bending angles Perriollat and Bartoli [2007], as depicted in Fig.4.6. The resulting model can then be fit to the image by minimizing the reprojection error of matching points in the reference and input images.

The fact that sheets of paper are developable surfaces has been extensively used in the document processing community, for example to synthetically flatten the images of curved documents and remove shadows. The resulting approaches do not necessarily rely on correspondences. Because of the very specific layout of printed pages, they can take advantage of shading Zhang et al. [2004] or of textural information Liang et al. [2005] to infer 3D shape.

4.2.2   SMOOTH SURFACES

While the methods that assume the surfaces to be developable may be effective in the specific context they have been designed for, they do not generalize naturally to broader classes of surface deformations such as those of cloth. One way to achieve such generalization is to replace the zero Gaussian curvature constraint by weaker ones that only force the curvature to remain small and the deformations to be smooth.

Such regularization constraints can be introduced by enforcing a uniform level of smoothness across the whole surface, which is simple to do but tends to preclude the modeling of sharp folds and creases. A powerful alternative is to only force the surface to be locally or piecewise smooth, which increases the algorithms' descriptive power at the cost of introducing slightly more complex models.

4.2.2.1   Global Smoothness

As discussed in Chapter 2, a well-known approach to enforcing smoothness is to regularize shape deformations with a linear subspace model. While, in essence, assuming that the shape is generated with a small number of deformation modes does not necessarily enforce smoothness, the usual ways of obtaining these modes, such as Modal Analysis or PCA of a reprentative set of deformed versions of

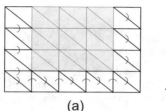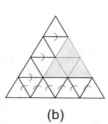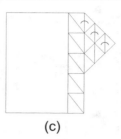

(a)   (b)   (c)

Figure 4.7: Specifying the 3D shape of a triangulated mesh. (a) We fix the shape of the bottom row from left to right by rotating each facet with respect to its left neighbor. For each following row, we only need to set the angle between the leftmost facet and the one below and the angle between the rightmost facet and its left neighbor. (b) The angles between the facets of the bottom row are first set from left to right. For each upper row, only the angle of the first facet need be set. (c) Attaching two hexagonal patches together. Because the base of each triangular patch is attached to the body, only one single angle is required to fully specify their first row.

the surface, typically yield smooth basis shapes representing low deformation frequencies. This makes sense because these techniques tend to be employed to create general purpose deformation modes. It is in contrast to the shape bases used by the NRSFM techniques that will be discussed in Chapter 6, which are recomputed for each new sequence and are not restricted to smooth deformations.

Under a linear subspace model, surface deformations are represented as linear combinations of a relatively small number of basis vectors. This can be expressed as

$$\mathbf{x} = \mathbf{x}_0 + \sum_{i=1}^{N_s} c_i \mathbf{s}_i = \mathbf{x}_0 + \mathbf{S}\mathbf{c} \, , \tag{4.6}$$

where $\mathbf{x}$ is the coordinate vector or Eq. 4.1, the $\mathbf{s}_i$ are the basis vectors, and the c_i their associated weights. $\mathbf{S}$ is a matrix whose columns are the $\mathbf{s}_i$ and $\mathbf{c}$ the vector of weights.

In the absence of either a stiffness matrix or sufficient amounts of training data, an approach to automatically generating deformed shapes was proposed in Salzmann *et al.* [2007c]. It relies on the fact that the shape of an inextensible triangulated mesh can be parameterized in terms of a small subset of the angles between its facets, as depicted by Fig. 4.7. Thus, given a reference shape represented as a triangulated mesh, a representative set of deformed shapes can be synthesized by randomly sampling this set of angles and generating the corresponding shapes. The resulting modes, computed via PCA, were shown to allow reconstructing very general deformable surfaces. In fact, it was observed that they produced better results than those obtained from a stiffness matrix computed using a finite element package when the exact physical parameters of the surface were not known and had to be guessed Salzmann [2009]. In practice, these modes have been used to reconstruct surfaces by optimizing their weights so as to minimize an objective function combining information provided by point correspondences, surface boundaries, and occluding contours. The resulting algorithm was

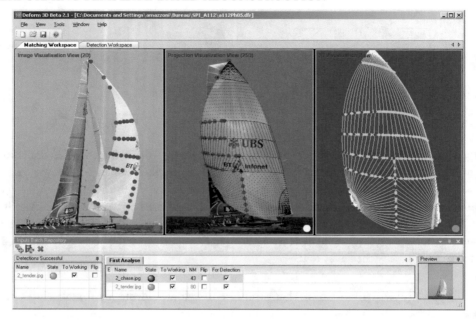

Figure 4.8: Screen capture of the semi-automated system that was delivered to Team Alinghi to compute the 3D shape of their sails after training sessions.

integrated into a semi-automated system, depicted by Fig. 4.8, that was designed to recover the 3D shape of sails and delivered to the Team Alinghi, the syndicate that won the America's Cup in 2003 and 2007. For a surface such as the one of Fig. 4.8 that is modeled by a 1200-vertex mesh, involving 3600 degrees of freedom, 30 to 40 modes are typically enough to model smooth deformations.

By reducing the number of variables to be optimized, the modal representation makes it easy to integrate additional information sources, which require the minimization of a nonlinear criterion. However, while effective, this kind of approach suffers from the fact that a non-convex objective function must be minimized and that, therefore, convergence to a desirable local optimum cannot be guaranteed. When using correspondences alone, this limitation can be removed as follows Salzmann *et al.* [2008a]. Recall that the 3D mesh representing the surface must be such that the vector $\mathbf{x}$ obtained by stacking the coordinates of its vertices must satisfy the linear system of Eq. 4.1. Injecting the formulation of Eq. 4.6 into Eq. 4.1 means that the weights $\mathbf{c}$ must be solution of

$$\mathbf{MSc} = -\mathbf{Mx}_0 \ .$$

$$(4.7)$$

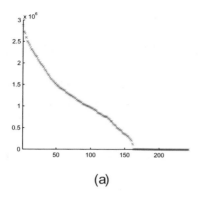

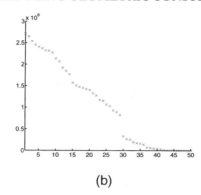

(a)   (b)

Figure 4.9: (a) Singular values of the linear system of Eq. 4.1 written in terms of the 243 vertex coordinates of a mesh. As mentioned in Chapter 3, the number of singular values close to zero is the number of vertices. (b) Describing the shape with 50 PCA modes helps constraining the corresponding linear system. However, there are still a number of near zero eigenvalues.

Since the vectors s_i are computed as eigenvectors of a covariance matrix, following standard practice in modal analysis, it then makes sense to solve

$$\begin{bmatrix} \mathbf{MS} & \mathbf{Mx}_0 \\ \lambda_r \mathbf{L} & \mathbf{0} \end{bmatrix} \begin{bmatrix} \mathbf{c} \\ 1 \end{bmatrix} = \mathbf{0} \, , \tag{4.8}$$

in the least squares sense, where $\mathbf{L}$ is a diagonal matrix whose elements are the inverse values of the eigenvalues associated to the eigenvectors, and λ_r is a regularization weight. This favors the modes that correspond to the lowest-frequency deformations and therefore further enforces smoothness.

In practice, the linear system of Eq. 4.8 is less poorly conditioned than the one of Eq. 4.1, but, as depicted by Fig. 4.9, its matrix still has a number of near zero singular values, indicating that there are several *smooth* shapes that all yield virtually the same projection. As a consequence, additional constraints still need to be imposed for the problem to become well-posed. We will see in Section 4.2.3 that forcing geodesic distances to be preserved across the surface in one way of doing this. Another is to exploit additional sources of image information, as discussed below.

In Salzmann *et al.* [2008a], it was proposed to treat the small singular values of Eq. 4.8 as if they were exactly zero and write potential solutions as linear combinations of the corresponding singular vectors. In other words, the mode weights can be written as

$$\mathbf{c} = \sum \beta_i \mathbf{m}_i \, , \tag{4.9}$$

where the $\mathbf{m}_i$ are the singular vectors associated to the smallest singular values of the matrix of Eq. 4.8. The unknowns become the weights β_i. Each set of weights produces a different 3D surface that projects at approximately the correct place in the input image. Therefore, additional information must be brought to bear to choose the best possible values of β_i.

When the surface can be assumed to be lit by a distant light source, these additional constraints can be obtained from shading information around corresponding points to constrain the intensities of surrounding surface patches in the input and reference images to be related through a Lambertian reflectance model Moreno-Noguer et al. [2009]. The shading information yields a system of cubic equations on the weights β_i. Since there are many such cubic constraints, they are solved by extended linearization Courtois et al. [2000]. While extended linearization does not guarantee an exact solution of the constraints, it is more practical than other techniques such as Groebner bases, which cannot handle that many equations. In Moreno-Noguer et al. [2010], the approach of Moreno-Noguer et al. [2009] was extended to allow the use of more generic shading models. Instead of writing the vector $\mathbf{c}$ as a weighted sum of singular vectors, the fact that solving the system of Eq. 4.7 is ill-conditioned was addressed as follows. The least-squares solution of Eq. 4.7 can be expressed as

$$\mathbf{c} = (\mathbf{B}^\top \mathbf{B})^{-1} \mathbf{B}^\top \mathbf{b} \; , \tag{4.10}$$

where $\mathbf{B} = \mathbf{MS}$ and $\mathbf{b} = -\mathbf{Mx}_0$. Recall from Chapter 3 that the coefficients of the matrix $\mathbf{M}$ of Eq. 4.1 are ultimately derived from point correspondences, which contain some amount of uncertainty. Assuming the image coordinates of these point correspondences to be normally distributed around their true values, the covariance matrix for the distribution of $\mathbf{c}$ can be expressed as

$$\Sigma_\mathbf{c} = \mathbf{J}_\beta \Sigma_\mathbf{u} \mathbf{J}_\beta^\top \; , \tag{4.11}$$

where

$$\mathbf{J}_\beta = \frac{\partial (\mathbf{B}^\top \mathbf{B})^{-1}}{\partial \mathbf{u}} \mathbf{B}^\top \mathbf{b} + (\mathbf{B}^\top \mathbf{B})^{-1} \frac{\partial \mathbf{B}^\top \mathbf{b}}{\partial \mathbf{u}} \tag{4.12}$$

is the Jacobian of $(\mathbf{B}^\top \mathbf{B})^{-1} \mathbf{B}^\top \mathbf{b}$ with respect to the 2D correspondence coordinates, which can be computed analytically. $\Sigma_\mathbf{u}$ is a diagonal covariance matrix representing the distribution of the 2D point coordinates around their true locations. The algorithm then samples the possible shapes around the mean shape given by the least-squares solution of Eq. 4.10 according to the covariance matrix $\Sigma_\mathbf{c}$ of Eq. 4.11. An additional source of information, such as motion or shading, is then used to evaluate the quality of the samples and resample the solution space more finely around the most promising ones. When using shading, a single light source whose position is unknown and may be either distant or nearby is assumed. For each sample $\mathbf{c}$, the light source position is estimated so that the image synthesized by shading the corresponding surface is as similar as possible to the original one. To speedup convergence, the samples for which this optimization yields the smallest residuals are favored in the resampling step. The fact that the algorithm provides a reliable way to generate 3D shape hypotheses makes the use of nearby light-sources practical. Without these hypotheses, such illumination conditions are difficult to handle, since they involve solving a non-convex minimization problem. This is all the more true since the lighting parameters are initially unknown and must be estimated from the images. In other words, while the lighting model used in Moreno-Noguer et al. [2010] is still too simple to be truly general, the approach could, in theory at least, handle much

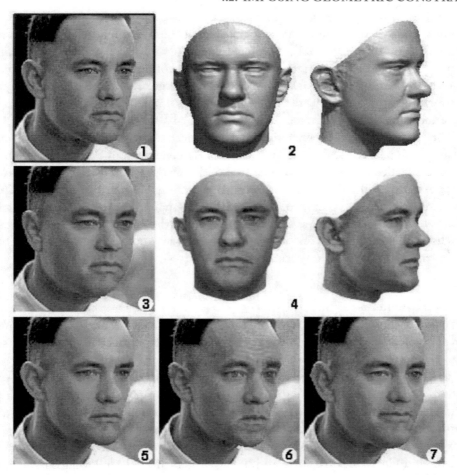

Figure 4.10: Matching a morphable model to a single sample image Blanz and Vetter [1999]. (1) of a face results in a 3D shape (2) and a texture map estimate. The texture estimate can be improved by additional texture extraction (4). The 3D model is rendered back into the image after changing facial attributes, such as gaining (3) and loosing weight (5), frowning (6), or being forced to smile (7). Courtesy of T. Vetter

more sophisticated ones and therefore use shading information more effectively than is currently done.

A different approach to combining texture and shading cues was proposed in White and Forsyth [2006]. Textural information is exploited by first triangulating the image and then computing normal estimates by template-matching the individual triangles against frontal reference views. This gives accurate normal information up to a two-fold normal ambiguity, which is resolved by using shading information and, when necessary, smoothness constraints. This approach uses more of the textural information than all those that rely solely on interest points, which ignore most of the image pixels. As discussed in Chapter 2, when operating in a well-defined domain such as face reconstruction for which there exists not only a geometric model but also an appearance model, it becomes possible to use the image texture even more extensively by using an analysis-by-synthesis approach Blanz and Vetter [1999], Romdhani and Vetter [2003] to estimate both shape and illumination parameters, as shown in Fig. 4.10.

While the mesh-based parameterization is the most common representation for template-based reconstruction, it is not the only possible one. As mentioned in Section 2.3, control points based parameterizations have been proposed to model non-rigid objects. Recently, in Brunet *et al.* [2010], a free-form deformation model was recently used for monocular reconstruction. This model has the advantage of making it easy to compute a global smoothness regularizer by exploiting the second derivatives of the B-spline basis functions that define the deformations. This regularizer used in conjunction with additional distance constraints was shown to outperform several state-of-the-art methods in terms of reconstruction accuracy.

4.2.2.2 Local Smoothness

The methods of Section 4.2.2.1, which rely on regularization models expressed as linear combinations of deformation modes, are good at recovering the shape of surfaces that deform relatively smoothly. However, they do not perform as well when deformations are more local or sharper, such as those depicted by Figs. 4.4 and 4.11 where folds appear on the surface. In theory, handling such local deformations could be achieved by using a much larger number of global modes. However, in practice, this would mean introducing far more variables—the weights associated to the modes—which, for computational reasons, could easily make the previous approaches impractical.

An approach to overcoming this problem by replacing global smoothness constraints with local ones was introduced in Salzmann *et al.* [2008b]. It starts from the following observations. First, locally, all parts of a physically homogeneous surface obey the same deformation rules. Second, these local deformations are more constrained than those of the global surface and can be learned from fewer examples. To exploit this, it is the manifold of local, as opposed to global, surface deformations that is represented. In Salzmann *et al.* [2008b], these local models were learned using a nonlinear technique. However, this yields non-convex objective functions, and is therefore only appropriate in a tracking framework. Thus, these nonlinear models were later replaced by linear ones, where each local patch is represented as a linear combination of modes Salzmann and Fua [2011].

In Salzmann and Fua [2011], this representation was used to regularize the reconstruction of the global surface by penalizing large local shape deviations from the learned linear manifold. To this end, as shown in Fig. 4.12, the mesh representing the surface is subdivided into overlapping patches. Each patch is taken as an $N_p \times N_p$ square mesh, with $N_p = 5$ in Salzmann and Fua [2011]. Note that this does not truly limit the approach to rectangular surfaces, since patches can be defined partially outside the global shape. Given an instance of a surface, each one of its local patches is

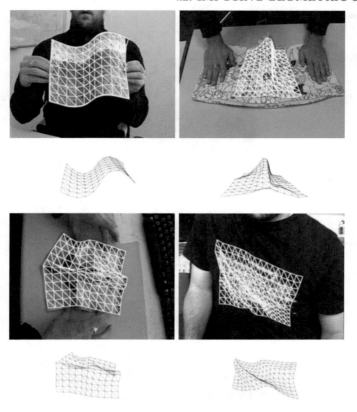

Figure 4.11: Reconstruction of deformable surfaces made of different materials undergoing complex deformations. In all four cases, we show the reconstructed 3D mesh overlaid on the input image and below a side view of the same mesh. © 2011 IEEE.

assigned a penalty proportional to its Mahalanobis distance to the mean shape. To avoid optimizing the individual patches independently, and therefore having to enforce consistency *a posteriori*, the technique exploits the fact that the local mode weights $\tilde{\mathbf{c}}$ can be directly obtained from the vertex coordinates as

$$\tilde{\mathbf{c}} = \tilde{\mathbf{S}}^T \left(\tilde{\mathbf{x}} - \tilde{\mathbf{x}}_0 \right) \, , \qquad (4.13)$$

where $\tilde{\mathbf{S}}$ is the matrix of local modes, and $\tilde{\mathbf{x}}$ is the vector containing the mesh vertices associated to a single patch. Note that this amounts to marginalizing out the mode weights, as is done in probabilistic PCA Tipping and Bishop [1999]. The resulting regularization term for a single patch can then be expressed as

$$\left\| \tilde{\mathbf{L}}^{1/2} \tilde{\mathbf{c}} \right\| = \left\| \tilde{\mathbf{L}}^{1/2} \mathbf{S}^T \left(\tilde{\mathbf{x}} - \tilde{\mathbf{x}}_0 \right) \right\|_2 \, , \qquad (4.14)$$

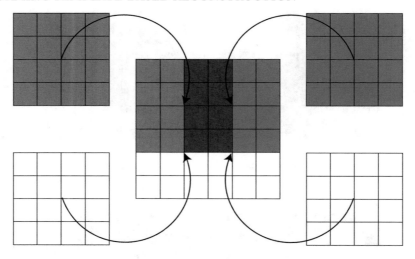

Figure 4.12:   Local deformation models. The surface mesh is divided into overlapping patches, whose deformations are modeled either as linear combinations of modes or in terms of a GPLVM. This can be used to represent surfaces of arbitrary shape or topology by adequately assembling local patches.

where $\tilde{\mathbf{L}}$ is the diagonal matrix containing the inverse eigenvalues associated with the eigenvectors in $\tilde{\mathbf{S}}$. As in the global case, this regularizer could be written as a linear system, and added as a penalty term to the correspondence equations of Eq. 4.1. Unfortunately, without additional constraints, linear local models suffer from the same shortcomings as global ones: Some of the singular values of the matrix of the resulting linear system remain small and additional knowledge must be introduced.

As a consequence, in Salzmann and Fua [2011], the shape regularization term of Eq. 4.14 was used in conjunction with the geodesic distance preservation constraints introduced in Section 4.2.3. An iterative scheme where each correspondence equation is re-weighted according to the current reprojection error allow the algorithm of Salzmann and Fua [2011] to tolerate up to 30% of erroneous correspondences between the reference and input image. This is enough in many practical applications, but may not suffice in truly difficult situations, such as when the texture is highly repetitive, as shown in Fig. 4.13. Reliable correspondences then become very difficult to establish because, based on image appearance alone, a 2D interest point in the reference image could match equally well any number of points in the input image. In Shaji *et al.* [2010], the problem is recast as one of simultaneously solving for shape and correspondences, which makes it possible to use geometrical consistency constraints when establishing the correspondences. As a result, when faced with a repetitive pattern such as the one of Fig. 4.13, it yields more reliable correspondences and, as a consequence, a better 3D shape. The approach starts with the formulation of Salzmann and Fua [2011] and extends it by allowing one point in the reference image to potentially correspond to more

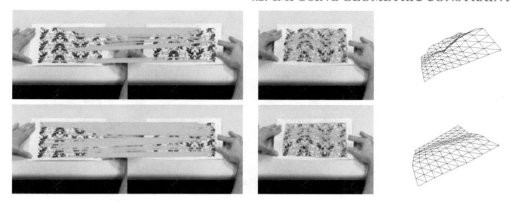

Figure 4.13:   Repetitive texture. **Top Row** The established correspondences between the reference and the target image, reconstructed 3D mesh reprojected into the target image, and the same mesh seen from a different viewpoint for the method of Salzmann and Fua [2011]. **Bottom Row** Similar outputs for the method of Shaji *et al.* [2010]. © 2010 IEEE.

than one point in the input image. This amounts to adding new lines in the matrix **M** of Eq. 4.1 and to introducing indicator variables that encode which ones of these correspondences are truly active. The quadratic problem of Salzmann and Fua [2011] becomes a mixed integer quadratic problem, which is NP-hard. Nevertheless, a branch-and-bound strategy was shown to yield good approximate solutions Shaji *et al.* [2010], at the cost of increased computational complexity with respect to Salzmann and Fua [2011]. In Sanchez-Riera *et al.* [2010], correspondences are also established simultaneously as the shape is recovered. In that case, given a shape prior modeled as a mixture of Gaussians, a strategy based on Kalman filtering is employed to progressively reduce the number of 2D point candidates that can be matched to a 3D point.

4.2.3   DISTANCE CONSTRAINTS

As discussed in Section 4.2.2, whether enforced locally or globally, smoothness by itself does not suffice to make the 3D monocular surface reconstruction problem well-posed and to guarantee a unique solution. Additional constraints are required. Enforcing distances across the deforming surface to be preserved has proved an effective way of disambiguating shape recovery.

In Salzmann *et al.* [2008a], reconstruction was performed under a global linear subspace model. The modal weights **c** were expressed as the weighted sum of Eq. 4.9 and the weights β_i became the unknowns of the problem. Overcoming the ambiguities left by the smoothness constraints was done by choosing the weights β_i that result in a surface in which the Euclidean distances between neighboring vertices remain as similar as possible to their value in the reference configuration. These constraints can be expressed as

$$\|\mathbf{v}_i - \mathbf{v}_j\|_2^2 = l_{i,j}^2 \ , \ \ \forall (i, j) \in \mathcal{E} \ , \tag{4.15}$$

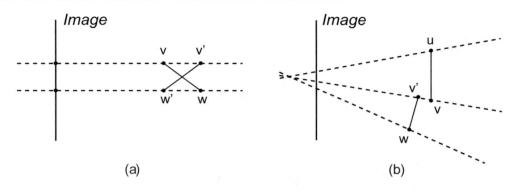

(a)   (b)

Figure 4.14: (a) Under orthographic projection, even when the average depth and length of a segment are known, the location of its 3D points is only determined up to a front to back reversal ambiguity. (b) Under perspective projection, knowing the length of a segment can be used to establish upper bounds on the depth of its points. Note that, for a point belonging to two segments, several disagreeing upper bounds can be obtained.

where $\mathcal{E}$ is the set of mesh edges. These constraints are quadratic in the $\mathbf{v}_i$, and thus in the β_i, but not convex. Furthermore, there are typically many of them—several thousands in the case of the mesh of Fig. 4.8—since there is one per edge of the mesh. As in Moreno-Noguer et al. [2009], extended linearization Courtois et al. [2000] is used to solve the resulting large quadratic system in terms of the β_i, from which the shape can then be computed. In Salzmann and Fua [2011], it was first suggested to exploit the same Euclidean distance constraints as in Salzmann et al. [2008a], and to rely on the same extended linearization technique, but using a local deformation model. In practice, however, using local instead of global models in this way does not significantly change the results as the surface is effectively prevented from developing sharp creases by the constraints.

Approaches to exploiting inextensibility constraints by considering distances between interest points on the surface instead of between mesh vertices have also been proposed. The one of Ecker et al. [2008] relies on the fact that, under orthographic projection, preserving the distance between two points constrains the segment linking them up to a potential front to back reversal, illustrated by Fig. 4.14(a). Reconstructing these segments whose orientation presents a binary ambiguity and regularizing them with a spline-based smoothness term amounts to solving a Semi Definite Programming problem, for which effective software tools exist Sturm [1999]. A similar philosophy is pursued in Perriollat et al. [2010] but in the full projective case. In that situation, forcing the distance between two feature points to remain constant can be used to establish upper bounds on their depth, as shown in Fig. 4.14(b). The surface reconstruction process starts by computing these bounds for all pairs of neighboring points, and iteratively refines them to make them consistent with each other. The resulting point cloud can be taken as the final solution, or can be smoothed by fitting a thin-plate spline to it. A strength of these approaches as compared to Salzmann et al. [2008a] is that, initially at least, no assumptions need be made about surface smoothness.

Figure 4.15: Demonstrating why constant Euclidean length constraints are ill-suited for sharp folds. Left: Two points of the discrete representation of a continuous surface in its rest configuration. Right: When the surface deforms, while the geodesic distance between the two points is preserved, the Euclidean one decreases. This suggests that distance inequality constraints should be used rather than equalities.

While preserving Euclidean distances has proved effective, it remains an approximation of the true physical behavior: What is truly preserved on a deforming inextensible surface is the *geodesic*, as opposed to Euclidean, distance between points. To be most effective, the techniques proposed in Ecker *et al.* [2008], Perriollat *et al.* [2010] therefore require relatively evenly placed feature points that can be detected and whose distance from each other is relatively small so that the Euclidean distance is a reasonable approximation of the geodesic one. This also true of the Salzmann *et al.* [2008a] approach, but this requirement is more readily satisfied since the distances constrained are those between neighboring mesh vertices, independently of the surface texture. As long as inter-vertex distances remain reasonably small with respect to the local radius of curvature, the requirement will be met.

As illustrated by Fig. 4.15, when creases develop on an inextensible surface, the Euclidean distance between vertices of the mesh representing it may decrease. It is the geodesic distance that remains constant and, in effect, bounds the Euclidean one. In Salzmann and Fua [2011], it was therefore proposed to replace the constant distance constraints of Ecker *et al.* [2008], Perriollat *et al.* [2010], Salzmann *et al.* [2008a] by inequality constraints that force the distance between neighboring vertices to remain smaller than their geodesic distance, which can be computed in the reference image. Because of scale ambiguities, these inequality constraints by themselves do not sufficiently constrain the solution as they do not prevent the mesh from globally shrinking. This is handled by adding a balloon force not unlike the one proposed in Cohen and Cohen [1993] that pushes the mesh away from the camera as far as possible without violating any of the constraints. All these constraints and forces can be expressed directly in terms of the mesh vertex coordinates, which results in an optimization problem of the form

$$\underset{\mathbf{X}}{\text{minimize}} \quad \|\mathbf{Mx}\|_2 + \|\Lambda(\mathbf{x} - \mathbf{x}_0)\|_2 - \lambda_d \mathbf{x}^T \mathbf{d} \qquad (4.16)$$
$$\text{subject to} \quad \|\mathbf{v}_k - \mathbf{v}_j\| \leq l_{j,k} \,, \ \forall (j,k) \in \mathcal{E} \,,$$

where $\mathbf{M}$ is the matrix of Eq. 4.1, Λ is a matrix that groups the regularization term of Eq. 4.14 for all patches, and $\mathbf{d}$ is the vector that encodes the balloon forces, which amount to maximizing the depth of surface points. w_d is a weight that controls the influence of the balloon forces relative to the magnitude of reprojection errors. This is a convex minimization problem that can be efficiently

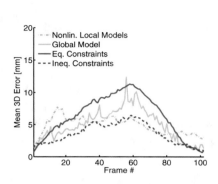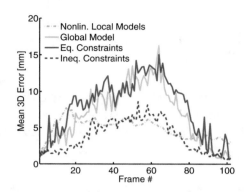

Figure 4.16: Mean vertex-to-vertex distance between reconstructions and ground-truth meshes. The reconstructions were obtained from synthetic correspondence (left) and SIFT correspondences (right). Results were obtained with the linear local models of Salzmann and Fua [2011] with distance equalities and inequalities, as well as with the nonlinear local models of Salzmann *et al.* [2008b] (green) and the global models of Salzmann *et al.* [2008a] with distance equalities (cyan). The largest deformation appears around frame 60, where the difference in accuracy is the greatest.

formulated as an SOCP problem by introducing slack variables Boyd and Vandenberghe [2004]. Doing so allows to re-write the problem as

$$\begin{aligned}
\underset{\mathbf{X}, \epsilon_c, \epsilon_r}{\text{minimize}} \quad & \epsilon_c + \epsilon_r - \lambda_d \mathbf{x}^T \mathbf{d} \\
\text{subject to} \quad & \|\mathbf{M}\mathbf{x}\|_2 \leq \epsilon_c , \\
& \|\Lambda(\mathbf{x} - \mathbf{x}_0)\|_2 \leq \epsilon_r , \\
& \|\mathbf{v}_k - \mathbf{v}_j\| \leq l_{j,k} , \quad \forall (j, k) \in \mathcal{E} ,
\end{aligned} \tag{4.17}$$

which, like the problem of Eq. 4.4, can be solved using a standard solver Sturm [1999]. As depicted by Fig. 4.16, the resulting solution of Salzmann and Fua [2011] tends to outperform the global smoothness methods of Salzmann *et al.* [2008a], as well as the nonlinear local models of Salzmann *et al.* [2008b].

While the optimization problem of Eq. 4.16 is convex, it also is very large and takes a long time to solve. As a result, this approach is ill-suited to real-time applications. One way to alleviate this problem is to leverage the availability of a good initial solution to exploit efficient least-squares resolution techniques. To this end, the problem of Eq. 4.16 can be reformulated as the constrained least-squares minimization problem

$$\begin{aligned}
\underset{\mathbf{X}}{\text{minimize}} \quad & \|\mathbf{M}\mathbf{x}\|_2^2 + \|\Lambda(\mathbf{x} - \mathbf{x}_0)\|_2^2 \\
\text{subject to} \quad & \|\mathbf{v}_k - \mathbf{v}_j\| = l_{j,k} , \quad \forall (j, k) \in \mathcal{E} .
\end{aligned} \tag{4.18}$$

Figure 4.17: Modeling the deformations of a main sail by minimizing an objective function under constraint. The black circles in the leftmost image are targets that can be automatically detected and were used to establish correspondences with the reference configuration. The algorithm can estimate the 3D deformations at a rate of approximately 10 Hz on a standard PC.

Note that, in this formulation, the length constraints are again equality constraints. Consequently, the balloon forces are no longer necessary and have been dropped. We will relax the constraints into inequalities below. Solving the problem of Eq. 4.18 is equivalent to solving in the least-squares sense

$$\mathbf{M}_\Lambda \mathbf{x} = \mathbf{b}_\Lambda \quad \text{subject to } \mathbf{e}(\mathbf{x}) = \mathbf{0}, \tag{4.19}$$

where $\mathbf{M}_\Lambda = [\mathbf{M}; \Lambda]$ is the matrix obtained by stacking up the lines of $\mathbf{M}$ and those of Λ, $\mathbf{b}_\Lambda = [\mathbf{0}; -\Lambda \mathbf{x}_o]$, and $\mathbf{e}(\mathbf{x})$ is the vector of deviations from the desired lengths. Its components are terms of the form $\|\mathbf{v}_k - \mathbf{v}_j\| - l_{j,k}$, one for each edge in $\mathcal{E}$.

Assuming the mesh contains N_v vertices and N_e edges, this constrained optimization problem involves $n = 3N_v$ variables and $m = N_e$ edge length constraints, with $m < n$ in all practical cases. It can therefore be solved very effectively using an iterative algorithm inspired by inverse kinematics approaches to solving underconstrained problems Baerlocher and Boulic [2004]. At each iteration, given the current state $\mathbf{x}$, the computation goes through the two following steps:

1. Project the n-dimensional $\mathbf{x}$ onto the space of constraints by finding $d\mathbf{x}$ such that

$$\mathbf{e}(\mathbf{x} + d\mathbf{x}) = 0 . \tag{4.20}$$

By doing a first-order Taylor approximation of the previous equation, we can write this projection as

$$\mathbf{A}d\mathbf{x} = -\mathbf{e}(\mathbf{x}) \Rightarrow d\mathbf{x} = -\mathbf{A}^\dagger \mathbf{e}(\mathbf{x}) + (\mathbf{I} - \mathbf{A}^\dagger \mathbf{A})\beta , \tag{4.21}$$

where $\mathbf{A}$ is the $m \times n$ Jacobian matrix of the m-dimensional constraint vector $\mathbf{e}(\mathbf{x})$, and $\mathbf{A}^\dagger$ its pseudo-inverse. β is an arbitrary n-dimensional vector that is projected into the null space of the linearized constraints by multiplying it by the matrix $\mathbf{P} = \mathbf{I} - \mathbf{A}^\dagger\mathbf{A}$, also known as the projector onto $\mathbf{A}$'s kernel. $d\mathbf{x}_0 = -\mathbf{A}^\dagger\mathbf{e}(\mathbf{x})$ is the minimum norm solution of Eq. 4.21. Given these notations, the $d\mathbf{x}$ of Eq. 4.21 can be written as

$$d\mathbf{x} = d\mathbf{x}_0 + \mathbf{P}\beta \ , \tag{4.22}$$

where β acts as the new unknown of the problem. This formulation reflects the fact that, because there are fewer constraints than variables, the projection is not unique. Since $m < n$, $\mathbf{A}^\dagger$ can be computed as $\lim_{\delta \to 0} \mathbf{A}^T(\mathbf{A}\mathbf{A}^T + \delta\mathbf{I})^{-1}$, which involves inverting an $m \times m$ matrix and can be done even if $\mathbf{A}\mathbf{A}^T$ itself is non invertible. When $m \ll n$, which is the case in practice, performing the inversion in m-dimensional rather than n-dimensional space helps reducing the computational cost.

2. To minimize the criterion of Eq. 4.19, β is taken to be the vector that yields a value of $\mathbf{x}$ that solves the equation $\mathbf{M}_\lambda\mathbf{x} = \mathbf{b}_\lambda$ in the least-squares sense. In other words, β is the least-squares solution of

$$\mathbf{M}_\lambda(\mathbf{x} + d\mathbf{x}_0 + \mathbf{P}\beta) = \mathbf{b}_\lambda \ , \tag{4.23}$$

or, equivalently,

$$\mathbf{M}_\lambda\mathbf{P}\beta = \mathbf{b}_\lambda - \mathbf{M}_\lambda(\mathbf{x} + d\mathbf{x}_0) \ . \tag{4.24}$$

Solving this equation yields a value of β that is used to increment $\mathbf{x}$ by $d\mathbf{x}_0 + \mathbf{P}\beta$. The resulting coordinate vector can then be used as the new current state, and $\mathbf{A}$ and $\mathbf{e}(\mathbf{x})$ can be recomputed.

The process stops when $d\mathbf{x}$ becomes small enough. For reconstructions such as those depicted by Fig. 4.17 where the deformations around the rest shapes are relatively small, the optimization typically converges to a local minimum in about 10 iterations, which allows for real-time performance. To account for larger deformations, the same procedure can be used in a frame-to-frame tracking context, where the initial solution in each frame is taken as the result of the previous one. This corresponds to the framework proposed in Shen et al. [2009], where the shape regularization term was dropped. As a result, the method of Shen et al. [2009] simply involves finding the displacement within the null-space of the linearized inextensibility constraints that minimizes the reprojection errors. This, unfortunately, is only possible when correspondences are well-spread over the whole surface. By contrast, combining the regularization and constraint terms in the above-mentioned way gives good results even when there are relatively few correspondences.

For the same reasons as those discussed in the context of the Salzmann and Fua [2011] approach and depicted by Fig. 4.15, even better results can be obtained by replacing the length equality constraints $\mathbf{e}(\mathbf{x}) = \mathbf{0}$ of Eq. 4.19 by inequality constraints of the form $\mathbf{e}(\mathbf{x}) \leq \mathbf{0}$. As before, this means that edge lengths can shrink but not extend beyond a certain value. This only involves a trivial modification of the algorithm above: At each iteration, only currently active constraints are taken into account in the computation of $\mathbf{e}(\mathbf{x})$ and its Jacobian $\mathbf{A}$. Shrinkage to a trivial solution can then be prevented by replacing the matrix Λ of Eq. 4.19 by a stiffness matrix chosen so that the regularization term $\|\Lambda(\mathbf{x} - \mathbf{x}_0)\|_2^2$ approximates the sum of the squares of second derivatives of the vector $(\mathbf{x} - \mathbf{x}_o)$, such as the one used in Fua and Leclerc [1995]. This term both penalizes non-smooth deformations and prevents scaling. Note that such a stiffness matrix also defines local geometric constraints, since it only encodes links between neighboring mesh vertices.

The constrained least-squares minimization method is effective and fast, but, due to its iterative nature and to the specific formulation of the regularization term, it requires an initial shape estimate that is not too different from the desired result. It is therefore well adapted either in a frame-to-frame tracking context, or to surfaces that deform relatively little so that the reference shape can be used to initialize the computation. For situation where a single image of a surface undergoing large deformations is given as input, it was recently shown that an initialization to this problem can be computed with a discriminative predictor Salzmann and Urtasun [2010].

The many different shape regularizers and constraints that have been discussed in this chapter have made it possible to design effective algorithms for monocular non-rigid template-based reconstruction. In particular, local smoothness used in conjunction with inequality constraints has proved able to recover the shape of surfaces undergoing complex deformations with folds and creases. The major drawback of these techniques arises from the fact that they require a reference image in which the shape of the surface is known. In the next chapters, we will discuss another class of methods that do not rely on this assumption.

CHAPTER 5

Formalizing Non-Rigid Structure from Motion

The template-based methods discussed in Chapter 4 are effective at resolving the ambiguities inherent to deformable surface 3D reconstruction from a single input image, given that another image in which the shape is known can be used as a reference. However, in practice, such a reference may not always be available and there is a need for methods that can operate without one.

One important approach to overcoming this limitation is to take advantage of the fact that tracking points over sequences can also be used to resolve ambiguities, without the need for a reference shape. This has long been known in the context of rigid shape recovery and exploited by Structure-from-Motion (SFM) algorithms, usually using a variant of the factorization method Tomasi and Kanade [1992]. Although initially studied in Ullman [1983], Non-Rigid Structure-from-Motion (NRSFM) as formulated by most recent methods was introduced in Bregler *et al.* [2000] and has been vigorously pursued since then.

As in the template-based case, we first start by describing the settings under which most NRSFM methods operate. We then present the most common NRSFM formulations and discuss their ambiguities.

5.1 PROBLEM DEFINITION

In contrast to template-based reconstruction, NRSFM does not rely on a reference image where the surface shape is known. Instead, it exploits the availability of multiple images of the object of interest, generally in the form of a video sequence. Note that these images are not acquired simultaneously, and, therefore, the shape of the object is different in each image. Given frame-to-frame 2D correspondences, which can be obtained as discussed in Section 3.2, NRSFM can be formulated as the problem of estimating the 3D locations of the individual feature points in each input image.

In NRSFM, the motion of the camera is explicitly modeled and taken as an additional unknown of the problem. As a consequence, 3D points need to be expressed in a common world coordinate system. Furthermore, in general, camera internal parameters are not assumed to be known. In the following analysis, we will consider the same two projection models as in the template-based case, which we redefine here for the reader's convenience.

We will first introduce a general formulation of NRSFM under a weak perspective, or affine, camera model. In this case, the projection of a 3D point $\mathbf{q}_i$ can be written as

$$d \begin{bmatrix} u_i \\ v_i \end{bmatrix} = \mathbf{R}\mathbf{q}_i + \mathbf{t} \,, \tag{5.1}$$

where $\mathbf{R}$ contains the first two rows of the full camera rotation matrix, and $\mathbf{t}$ is the 2×1 camera translation vector. Assuming no distortion, the matrix of internal camera parameters reduces to a single focal length, which was here absorbed by the scalar d. Since, in NRSFM, the notion of facet is absent, the same d is used for all the points. We will then discuss NRSFM under full perspective projection, where the projection of a 3D point $\mathbf{q}_i$ is expressed as

$$d_i \begin{bmatrix} u_i \\ v_i \\ 1 \end{bmatrix} = \mathbf{A} \left(\mathbf{R}\mathbf{q}_i + \mathbf{t} \right) \,, \tag{5.2}$$

with $\mathbf{A}$ the 3×3 matrix of internal camera parameters.

As in the case of template-based reconstruction, correspondences alone are insufficient for unambiguous reconstruction. To reduce the ambiguities, most NRSFM methods rely on a linear subspace model to constrain the deformations of the 3D points. Whereas in the template-based case, the deformation modes could be infered from the reference mesh using a technique such as Salzmann et al. [2007c], this is no longer the case for NRSFM. Consequently, the modes are typically taken as additional unknown variables and recovered at the same time as their coefficients, along with the rotation and translation for each frame of the sequence. Note that, since the modes are obtained neither from a large dataset of deformed surfaces as in Salzmann et al. [2007c] nor by modal analysis, they do not necessarily favor smooth deformations. Depending on the number of basis shapes involved, they rather encourage the deformations to remain simple. Since most NRSFM techniques exploit this linear subspace representation, we will describe it as part of the general approach. However, as will be discussed in Chapter 6, some very recent methods depart significantly from this initial formulation.

In theory, NRSFM is more generally applicable than template-based shape recovery, since it requires neither a calibrated camera, nor a reference template. In practice, however, because of the higher number of degrees-of-freedom, NRSFM methods are subject to more ambiguities and are more sensitive to measurement noise. As a consequence, to be as effective as template-based approaches, they often require stronger constraints and a good initialization. In many cases, the latter is obtained by applying a rigid structure-from-motion algorithm.

In the remainder of this chapter, we start by reviewing the problem formulation for the weak perspective case as introduced in Bregler et al. [2000]. We then discuss NRSFM in the perspective case, as proposed by Hartley and Vidal [2008], Xiao and Kanade [2005].

5.2   NRSFM UNDER WEAK PERSPECTIVE PROJECTION

Recall from Eq. 5.1 that under the weak perspective model, the projection of a 3D point $\mathbf{q}_i$ can be written as

$$\begin{bmatrix} u_i \\ v_i \end{bmatrix} = \frac{1}{d}(\mathbf{R}\mathbf{q}_i + \mathbf{t}) , \tag{5.3}$$

where $\mathbf{R}$ contains the first two rows of a full rotation matrix, $\mathbf{t}$ is a 2×1 translation vector, and d is a scalar.

Given N_c such 3D points on a surface, the corresponding equations can be grouped in matrix form, which yields the system of equations

$$\begin{bmatrix} u_1 & \cdots & u_{N_c} \\ v_1 & \cdots & v_{N_c} \end{bmatrix} = \frac{1}{d}(\mathbf{R}\mathbf{Q} + \mathbf{T}) , \tag{5.4}$$

where $\mathbf{Q}$ is the $3 \times N_c$ matrix of 3D point coordinates, and $\mathbf{T}$ is the $2 \times N_c$ translation matrix whose columns all contain the same vector $\mathbf{t}$. Without loss of generality, and as was proposed in the factorization algorithm of Tomasi and Kanade Tomasi and Kanade [1992], the translation $\mathbf{T}$ can be eliminated by subtracting the mean of all 2D points, which is equivalent to assuming that the shape is centered at the origin. This also removes the translation ambiguity mentioned in Aanaes and Kahl [2002].

A standard assumption of NRSFM methods is that the shape can be approximated with a linear subspace model, meaning that the shape can be expressed as a linear combination of N_s basis shapes. Under this model, Eq. 5.4 can be re-written as

$$\begin{bmatrix} u_1 & \cdots & u_{N_c} \\ v_1 & \cdots & v_{N_c} \end{bmatrix} = \mathbf{R} \sum_{k=1}^{N_s} c_k \mathbf{S}_k , \tag{5.5}$$

where each $\mathbf{S}_k$ is a $3 \times N_c$ matrix containing one basis shape, and c_k is its associated coefficient. Note that since no mesh representation is available here, the basis shapes will depend on the specific configuration of feature points on the surface. Therefore, they cannot be pre-computed as in Chapter 4 and must be recovered together with their coefficients. Note also that, without loss of generality, the scalar d has been absorbed in the shape coefficients.

Given outlier-free frame-to-frame correspondences between the 2D surface features in an N_f frame video sequence, we can write Eq. 5.5 for each frame, and group all the resulting equations in a system of the form

$$\underbrace{\begin{bmatrix} u_1^1 & \cdots & u_{N_c}^1 \\ v_1^1 & \cdots & v_{N_c}^1 \\ \vdots & \vdots & \vdots \\ u_1^{N_f} & \cdots & u_{N_c}^{N_f} \\ v_1^{N_f} & \cdots & v_{N_c}^{N_f} \end{bmatrix}}_{\mathbf{W}} = \underbrace{\begin{bmatrix} c_1^1 \mathbf{R}^1 & \cdots & c_{N_s}^1 \mathbf{R}^1 \\ \vdots & \vdots & \vdots \\ c_1^{N_f} \mathbf{R}^{N_f} & \cdots & c_{N_s}^{N_f} \mathbf{R}^{N_f} \end{bmatrix}}_{\mathbf{C}} \underbrace{\begin{bmatrix} \mathbf{S}_1 \\ \vdots \\ \mathbf{S}_{N_s} \end{bmatrix}}_{\mathbf{B}} , \tag{5.6}$$

where $\mathbf{W}$ is the $2N_f \times N_c$ measurement matrix, $\mathbf{C}$ is a $2N_f \times 3N_s$ matrix, and $\mathbf{B}$ is the $3N_s \times N_c$ matrix containing the shape basis. In general, we expect $3N_s < 2N_f$ and $3N_s < N_c$. Therefore, $\mathbf{W}$ should have rank $3N_s$. In practice, because of measurement noise, $\mathbf{W}$ usually has full rank. However, its practical rank can be obtained by finding a significant drop in its singular values. This also gives a practical solution to the problem of estimating the number of basis shapes N_s.

Since $\mathbf{W}$ is directly obtained from the video sequence, a typical solution to obtaining $\mathbf{C}$ and $\mathbf{B}$ is by singular value decomposition. The left-singular vectors corresponding to the largest $3N_s$ singular values are taken as an estimate $\hat{\mathbf{C}}$ of $\mathbf{C}$, and the corresponding right-singular vectors as an estimate $\hat{\mathbf{B}}$ of $\mathbf{B}$. As will be discussed in Section 5.4, this decomposition is not unique, and additional constraints are required to obtain meaningful estimates. Given $\hat{\mathbf{C}}$, the rotation matrices and shape coefficients in each frame can be recovered individually. This is done by re-ordering and re-writing the rows $\hat{\mathbf{c}}^j$ of $\hat{\mathbf{C}}$ corresponding to frame j as

$$
\hat{\mathbf{c}}^j = \begin{bmatrix} c_1^j r_1^j & c_1^j r_2^j & c_1^j r_3^j & c_1^j r_4^j & c_1^j r_5^j & c_1^j r_6^j \\ & & & \vdots & & \\ c_{N_s}^j r_1^j & c_{N_s}^j r_2^j & c_{N_s}^j r_3^j & c_{N_s}^j r_4^j & c_{N_s}^j r_5^j & c_{N_s}^j r_6^j \end{bmatrix}, \tag{5.7}
$$

where $r_1^j, ..., r_6^j$ are the coefficients in the rotation matrix for frame j taken row-wise. This matrix can then be decomposed into

$$
\hat{\mathbf{c}}^j = \begin{bmatrix} c_1^j \\ \vdots \\ c_{N_s}^j \end{bmatrix} \begin{bmatrix} r_1^j & r_2^j & r_3^j & r_4^j & r_5^j & r_6^j \end{bmatrix}, \tag{5.8}
$$

which can be done by singular value decomposition. Note that, as for the decomposition of $\mathbf{W}$ into $\mathbf{C}$ and $\mathbf{B}$, this decomposition is not unique and need to be corrected to ensure that the r_i^j truly form a rotation matrix.

5.3   NRSFM UNDER FULL PERSPECTIVE PROJECTION

While the weak perspective camera model can be sufficient when the variation in depth over the whole object is fairly small, it is known that the full perspective model is often truer to what is observed in real images. Therefore, several authors have proposed NRSFM formulations for the full perspective case Bartoli *et al.* [2008], Hartley and Vidal [2008], Llado *et al.* [2010], Vidal and Abretske [2006], Wang and Wu [2010], Xiao and Kanade [2005]. Here, we derive the main equations underlying these techniques and describe the different approaches introduced to solving them.

Recall from Eq. 5.2 that the projection under the perspective camera model of a 3D point $\mathbf{q}_i$ represented by its homogeneous coordinates $\tilde{\mathbf{q}}_i = [\mathbf{q}_i^T, 1]^T$ can be written as

$$d_i \begin{bmatrix} u_i \\ v_i \\ 1 \end{bmatrix} = \mathbf{P}\tilde{\mathbf{q}}_i , \quad \mathbf{P} = \mathbf{A}[\mathbf{R}|\mathbf{t}] , \qquad (5.9)$$

where $\mathbf{A}$ is the matrix of internal camera parameters, $\mathbf{R}$ is the camera rotation matrix, and $\mathbf{t}$ is the camera translation vector. Although $\mathbf{A}$ is often assumed to be unknown, calibrating the camera better constrains the problem Hartley and Vidal [2008]. Recall that unlike in the weak perspective case, the scalar accounting for depth d_i is different for every point i.

As before, we can group in matrix form the equations corresponding to N_c such points found in a single frame, which yields

$$\begin{bmatrix} d_1 u_1 & \cdots & d_{N_c} u_{N_c} \\ d_1 v_1 & \cdots & d_{N_c} v_{N_c} \\ d_1 & \cdots & d_{N_c} \end{bmatrix} = \mathbf{P}\,\tilde{\mathbf{Q}} , \qquad (5.10)$$

where $\tilde{\mathbf{Q}}$ is the $4 \times N_c$ matrix of homogeneous point coordinates. By assuming again that the shape can be described as a linear combination of basis shapes $\mathbf{S}_k$, we can re-write the previous system as

$$\begin{bmatrix} d_1 u_1 & \cdots & d_{N_c} u_{N_c} \\ d_1 v_1 & \cdots & d_{N_c} v_{N_c} \\ d_1 & \cdots & d_{N_c} \end{bmatrix} = \mathbf{A}\mathbf{R} \sum_{k=1}^{N_s} c_k \mathbf{S}_k + \mathbf{A}\mathbf{T} , \qquad (5.11)$$

where we have explicitly decomposed the projection matrix into internal parameters, rotation and translation, and where each column of $\mathbf{T}$ contains the translation vector $\mathbf{t}$.

From the outlier-free correspondences between points in N_f frames, we can build the system of equations representing all projections of all points as

$$\underbrace{\begin{bmatrix} d_1^1 u_1^1 & \cdots & d_{N_c}^1 u_{N_c}^1 \\ d_1^1 v_1^1 & \cdots & d_{N_c}^1 v_{N_c}^1 \\ d_1^1 & \cdots & d_{N_c}^1 \\ \vdots & \vdots & \vdots \\ d_1^{N_f} u_1^{N_f} & \cdots & d_{N_c}^{N_f} u_{N_c}^{N_f} \\ d_1^{N_f} v_1^{N_f} & \cdots & d_{N_c}^{N_f} v_{N_c}^{N_f} \\ d_1^{N_f} & \cdots & d_{N_c}^{N_f} \end{bmatrix}}_{\mathbf{W}} = \underbrace{\begin{bmatrix} c_1^1 \mathbf{A}\mathbf{R}^1 & \cdots & c_{N_s}^1 \mathbf{A}\mathbf{R}^1 & \mathbf{A}\mathbf{t}^1 \\ \vdots & \vdots & \vdots & \vdots \\ c_1^{N_f} \mathbf{A}\mathbf{R}^{N_f} & \cdots & c_{N_s}^{N_f} \mathbf{A}\mathbf{R}^{N_f} & \mathbf{A}\mathbf{t}^{N_f} \end{bmatrix}}_{\mathbf{C}} \underbrace{\begin{bmatrix} \mathbf{S}_1 \\ \vdots \\ \mathbf{S}_{N_s} \\ 1 \end{bmatrix}}_{\mathbf{B}} , \qquad (5.12)$$

where $\mathbf{W}$ is the $3N_f \times N_c$ matrix of scaled measurements, $\mathbf{C}$ is a $3N_f \times (3N_s + 1)$ matrix, and $\mathbf{B}$ is the $(3N_s + 1) \times N_c$ matrix containing the shape basis.

Unfortunately, while in the weak perspective case $\mathbf{W}$ was known, here it depends on the unknown perspective depth scalars d_i^j. As a consequence, the solution cannot be directly estimated by a simple singular value decomposition. To overcome this difficulty, several solutions have been proposed. In Xiao and Kanade [2005], an iterative procedure was introduced to alternatively compute the structure and motion from fixed depths, and vice-versa. Initially, the depths d_i^j were set to 1. In Llado *et al.* [2010], some parts of the surface were assumed to move rigidly. Therefore, an initial solution was computed using the results obtained with a rigid structure from motion techniques on these parts and refined using a nonlinear optimization method. Recently, in Hartley and Vidal [2008], it was shown that the solution to perspective NRSFM could be obtained in closed-form by exploiting the tensor estimation and factorization method of Hartley and Schaffalitzky [2004]. While this gives an exact solution in the noise-free case, the approach is sensitive to noise. As observed in Hartley and Vidal [2008], this is mainly due to the fact that the tensor estimation and factorization method they relied on Hartley and Schaffalitzky [2004] lacks robustness to noise, as many purely algebraic methods do.

5.4   AMBIGUITIES OF NRSFM

Even though, in many NRSFM methods, the shape is already regularized by a linear subspace model, ambiguities remain. This makes sense, since the shape basis also is an unknown of the problem. Furthermore, while for template-based reconstruction going from weak to full perspective theoretically yields a better-posed problem, perspective NRSFM still suffers from the same ambiguities as the weak persective formulation.

First, the decomposition of $\mathbf{W}$ into $\mathbf{C}$ and $\mathbf{B}$ can only be computed up to an invertible transformation. Indeed, for any invertible $3N_s \times 3N_s$ matrix $\mathbf{G}$, we can write

$$\mathbf{W} = \hat{\mathbf{C}}\mathbf{G}\mathbf{G}^{-1}\hat{\mathbf{B}} = \mathbf{C}\mathbf{B} . \tag{5.13}$$

This was also observed for the rigid structure-from-motion problem in the factorization method of Tomasi and Kanade [1992]. This matrix $\mathbf{G}$ is known as the corrective transformation. Since, in theory, any $\mathbf{G}$ would do, a way must be found to choose the best one. Typically, this is done by finding a $\mathbf{G}$ that ensures that the rotation matrices are orthonormal. Details on the different manners to exploit this will be given in Chapter 6. In Xiao and Kanade [2004], Xiao *et al.* [2004b], it was argued that, even when enforcing orthonormality constraints, ambiguities remained in the reconstruction. However, it was later shown in Akhter *et al.* [2009] that all solutions in this ambiguous space yield equal structures up to a 3D rotation.

In addition to the corrective transformation, other ambiguities inherent to NRSFM were discussed in Aanaes and Kahl [2002]. One of them is the relative translation and scale between the camera center and the object. As in the template-based case of Chapter 3, it is impossible to differentiate between a fixed camera seeing an expanding object and a camera moving closer to a constant-size object. This, in general, is overcome either by fixing the object scale, or by imposing temporal smoothness. Similarly, there also is an ambiguity between the magnitude of the basis shapes and their corresponding coefficients.

Furthermore, the same global rotation-translation ambiguity as in the rigid case remains in non-rigid structure from motion solutions. In the full perspective case, it was shown in Hartley and Vidal [2008] that, in the uncalibrated case, the solution is only determined up to a linear transformation. However, with a calibrated camera, this ambiguity reduces to the same undetermined global rotation as in the weak perspective case.

Finally, in addition to the ambiguities inherent to the problem that have been formally proved in the above-mentioned papers, other ambiguities have been observed in practice. In Torresani et al. [2003], it was noted that if too many basis shapes were required, the reconstruction problem became ambiguous. Similarly, in Bartoli et al. [2008], the problem that treating all modes equally results in ambiguities due to the potential dependencies of the modes. Solutions to these problem involving higher order deformation models, or coarse-to-fine modes computation will be discussed in Chapter 6.

5.5   THE MISSING DATA PROBLEM

A weakness of non-rigid structure-from-motion techniques is their sensitivity to missing data and mismatches. Several solutions to these problems have been proposed.

The first publications to address the missing data problem were Brand [2001], Torresani et al. [2001]. Both proposed to exploit fully tracked points to infer the missing data. In particular, they follow the idea introduced by Irani [1999] for optical flow estimation, and establish a basis flow using the fully tracked points. More specifically, assuming that W has rank r, all columns of W can be modeled as linear combinations of r basis tracks. If at least r points have been tracked throughout the whole sequence, this basis can be obtained by singular value decomposition of the corresponding part of W. To fill in the missing data in matrix W, they follow the formulation of Lucas and Kanade [1981], and express the locations of the image points in terms of the basis coefficients. The resulting system of equations is then solved iteratively to obtain the correct coefficients and thus predict the location of points that were lost during tracking.

While this is effective when some points have been tracked in all images, it would still fail in the more realistic case where points are visible for some frames and then disappear. In Olsen and Bartoli [2008], this problem was addressed by separating the sequence into blocks of frames whose motion parameters can then be estimated. Given the motion in the individual blocks, the basis shapes can be estimated later by exploiting priors.

A different line of works followed the idea introduced in Marques and Costeira [2009] to deal with missing data in rigid structure-from-motion. In this paper, it was noted that rigid SFM with missing data can become ambiguous when the available points are in a degenerate configuration, such as on a plane. To overcome this issue, the authors introduced the notion of *motion manifold*, which constrains the recovered motion to be feasible. The available tracks can then be projected on this manifold, which makes reconstruction robust to those degenerate scenarios. In Paladini et al. [2009], this was extended to reconstruction of deformable and articulated objects seen under orthographic projection. Other methods were proposed in Del Bue et al. [2010], Wang et al. [2008] to allow for different camera models, as well as to improve the convergence properties of the original algorithm.

The above-mentioned techniques were designed to cope with missing data. A different problem arises from the presence of mismatches in the point tracks. To overcome these outliers, the most common scheme is to rely on a RANSAC Fischler and Bolles [1981] procedure Olsen and Bartoli [2008], Zhu et al. [2010]. Another solution involves using a robust estimator to weight the points according to the uncertainty of the measurements Shaji and Chandran [2008]. This technique also deals with missing data by assigning a zero weight to the lost points.

In any event, even though there are techniques designed to overcome the missing data problem, the theoretical solutions discussed in this chapter are not sufficiently constrained to recover meaningful structure and motion by themselves. As for template-based reconstruction, additional knowledge needs to be introduced in NRSFM algorithms. In the next chapter, we will discuss the different types of knowledge that have been proposed so far.

CHAPTER 6

Performing Non-Rigid Structure from Motion

In the previous chapter, we have shown that recovering non-rigid structure and motion from N_c points tracked in N_f frames could theoretically be done by factorizing a measurement matrix into a product of two matrices. This can be expressed as

$$\mathbf{W} = \mathbf{C}\mathbf{B} \,, \tag{6.1}$$

where $\mathbf{W}$ is the measurement matrix, $\mathbf{C}$ contains products of the shape coefficients with the motion parameters, and $\mathbf{B}$ contains the shape basis. However, as mentioned in Section 5.4, this factorization is subject to ambiguities. The decomposition can only be computed up to an invertible transformation $\mathbf{G}$, up to a global scale, and up to ambiguities between shape coefficient values and basis shape magnitudes. In addition to those theoretical ambiguities, the problem also is ill-conditioned due to the presence of image noise. As a consequence, constraints must be incorporated into the factorization to overcome these issues.

In general, adding constraints to the factorization of Eq. 6.1, yields an optimization problem that can be parameterized in two different ways. The first one involves expressing the reconstruction in terms of the corrective transform $\mathbf{G}$ only. This implicitly satisfies the measurement constraints, since $\mathbf{W} = \hat{\mathbf{C}}\hat{\mathbf{B}} = \hat{\mathbf{C}}\mathbf{G}\mathbf{G}^{-1}\hat{\mathbf{B}}$, where $\hat{\mathbf{C}}$ and $\hat{\mathbf{B}}$ are the matrices obtained by SVD. Therefore, only the additional regularization terms are taken into account to find the best $\mathbf{G}$. The second way is to write the objective in terms of the original variables $\mathbf{S}_k$, c_k^j, and $\mathbf{R}^j$ of Eqs. 5.6 or 5.12, as well as $\mathbf{A}$ and $\mathbf{t}^j$ if also optimized. This yields an optimization problem of the form

$$\underset{\mathbf{S}_k, c_k^j, \mathbf{R}^j}{\text{minimize}} \left\| \mathbf{W} - \mathbf{C}(c_k^j, \mathbf{R}^j)\mathbf{B}(\mathbf{S}_k) \right\|_F^2 \,, \tag{6.2}$$

where $\mathbf{C}$ and $\mathbf{B}$ are expressed as functions of the variables, and $\| \cdot \|_F$ is the Frobenius norm. Additional knowledge can then be introduced either as hard constraints or as regularizers in the objective function.

In this chapter, we review the different kinds of additional constraints that have been proposed in recent years. As in the case of template-based reconstruction, temporal and geometric consistency constraints have been used. In addition to these, an NRSFM-specific constraint arises from the fact that the estimated rotation matrices must be orthonormal. We will start with this one and then move on to temporal and geometric ones. Note that we do not differentiate between the weak and full perspective cases, since these constraints generally apply to both.

6.1   ORTHONORMALITY CONSTRAINTS

The first natural constraints that have been used to disambiguate NRSFM are orthonormality constraints Bregler *et al.* [2000]. As in rigid structure from motion Tomasi and Kanade [1992], they were introduced to encode the fact that the rotation matrices are orthonormal. Therefore, the goal is to find the invertible corrective transformation $\mathbf{G}$ that satisfies this property.

More specifically, from the formulation of Eq. 5.6, one can write orthonormality constraints for each of the individual blocks of $\mathbf{C}$. This yields equations of the form

$$\hat{\mathbf{C}}_{2j-1:2j}\mathbf{G}_k\mathbf{G}_k^T\hat{\mathbf{C}}_{2j-1:2j}^T = (c_k^j)^2\mathbf{R}^j\mathbf{R}^{j^T} = (c_k^j)^2\mathbf{I}_{2\times2} \, , \ 1 \leq j \leq N_f \, , \ 1 \leq k \leq N_s \, , \qquad (6.3)$$

where $\hat{\mathbf{C}}_{2j-1:2j}$ is a $2 \times 3N_s$ matrix containing the two consecutive rows of $\hat{\mathbf{C}}$ corresponding to frame j, $\mathbf{G}_k$ is a $3N_s \times 3$ matrix containing three consecutive columns of $\mathbf{G}$, and c_k^j is the weight of the kth basis shape in frame j. These constraints are quadratic in $\mathbf{G}$, and typically need to be solved by nonlinear optimization methods.

In the closed-form solution of Xiao *et al.* [2004b], the authors proposed an approach to making this step easier. To this end, they introduced new variables $\mathbf{H}_k = \mathbf{G}_k\mathbf{G}_k^T$. Given these quadratic variables, the constraints are re-written as

$$\hat{\mathbf{C}}_{2j-1}\mathbf{H}_k\hat{\mathbf{C}}_{2j-1}^T - \hat{\mathbf{C}}_{2j}\mathbf{H}_k\hat{\mathbf{C}}_{2j}^T \ = \ 0 \, , \ 1 \leq j \leq N_f \, , \ 1 \leq k \leq N_s \, , \qquad (6.4)$$

$$\hat{\mathbf{C}}_{2j-1}\mathbf{H}_k\hat{\mathbf{C}}_{2j}^T \ = \ 0 \, , \ 1 \leq j \leq N_f \, , \ 1 \leq k \leq N_s \, . \qquad (6.5)$$

The first constraint encodes both diagonal terms of Eq. 6.3 simultaneously, thus removing the dependency on the unknown coefficients c_k^j. The second constraint represents the off-diagonal terms. Only one such constraint needs to be added since $\mathbf{H}_k$ can be made implicitly symmetric, which makes both off-diagonal terms identical.

Unfortunately, it was shown in Xiao *et al.* [2004b] that this linearized version of the orthonormality constraints is not sufficient to fully disambiguate the reconstruction problem. This led the authors to argue that orthonormality constraints were insufficient on their own. However, as was suggested in Brand [2005] and later proved in Akhter *et al.* [2009], under noise-free observations, orthonormality constraints are sufficient to overcome the corrective transformation ambiguity of NRSFM. The reason for the remaining ambiguities found in Xiao *et al.* [2004b] was that no constraint was added to force the rank of $\mathbf{H}_k$ to be 3. In Akhter *et al.* [2009], it was shown that this additional rank constraint was sufficient to determine the structure. More specifically, $\mathbf{G}_k$ can still only be determined up to a Euclidean transformation, but this ambiguity has no influence on the reconstructed structure. This is depicted in Fig. 6.1, which illustrates the fact that a family of shapes satisfies the orthonormality constraints, but that any point in this region gives the same structure up to a 3D rotation.

While orthonormality constraints were shown to be sufficient to resolve ambiguities, solving the true constraints still involves a nonlinear optimization problem, which can lead to undesirable local minima. Several approaches to tackling this problem were proposed. For instance,

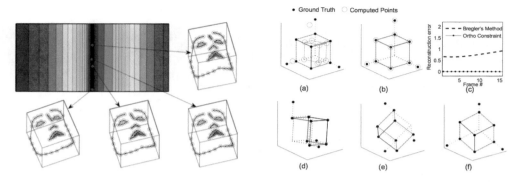

Figure 6.1: Ambiguities of orthonormality constraints Akhter *et al.* [2009]. (Left) Reconstruction of a face. The cost function suggests that many shapes satisfy orthonormality constraints. However, the shapes in this region are all the same up to a Euclidean transformation. (Right) Reconstruction of a cube from noise-free data. While the method of Bregler *et al.* [2000] does not give a correct solution (a), using orthonormality constraints gives a perfect reconstruction (b). As before, there exist several solutions, but they are all the same up to a global rotation (d-f). Courtesy of I. Akhter. © 2009 IEEE.

in Torresani *et al.* [2001], the authors relied on an iterative scheme that involved alternatively optimizing rotations, shape basis, and shape coefficients. Orthonormality constraints were implicitly satisfied by parameterizing the rotations with exponential coordinates. For similar reasons, in Llado *et al.* [2010], the rotations were parameterized with quaternions. By contrast, in Brand [2005] it was proposed to directly minimize the squared error induced by the orthonormality constraints of Eq. 6.3. A variable-metric quasi-Newton scheme was used and the constraint $\|\mathbf{G}_k\|_F = 1$ was added. In a similar constrained optimization paradigm, an algorithm that enforced orthonormality by constraining the solution to remain on a Riemannian manifold was developed in Shaji and Chandran [2008]. Fig. 6.2 depicts the results obtained with this method on the shark sequence of Torresani *et al.* [2008], which is used in many publications.

Despite the fact that orthonormality constraints strongly reduce the ambiguities of NRSFM, resulting solutions often remain sensitive to image noise. As a consequence, additional constraints need to be introduced. These constraints can be roughly classified into temporal consistency and geometric constraints, both of which are discussed below.

6.2   IMPOSING TEMPORAL CONSISTENCY

As shown in Chapter 4 for template-based reconstruction, accounting for the fact that, in a video sequence, the shape does not vary arbitrarily from frame to frame gives very strong reconstruction cues. This kind of knowledge is even better adapted to NRSFM, since it is specifically designed to deal with sequences as opposed to single frames. As a consequence, various types of temporal constraints have been proposed to improve structure and motion recovery.

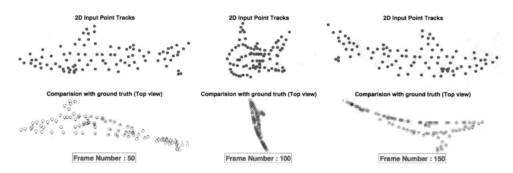

Figure 6.2: Reconstruction of the shark data using the method of Shaji and Chandran [2008]. Here, orthonormality is enforced by constraining the solution to remain on a Riemannian manifold. Red circles correspond to ground-truth points, and blue dots to reconstructed ones. Courtesy of S. Chandran. © 2009 IEEE.

In Section 4.1, we showed that zeroth order motion models are effective to constrain template-based frame-to-frame reconstruction. This remains true in NRSFM, where they have been used extensively Aanaes and Kahl [2002], Del Bue et al. [2007], Rabaud and Belongie [2008]. The intuition behind such models simply is that the variation of the shape $\mathbf{Q} = \sum_k c_k \mathbf{S}_k$ between two consecutive frames is small. Therefore, the term

$$\lambda_s \sum_{i=1}^{N_c} \sum_{j=2}^{N_f} \|\mathbf{Q}_i^j - \mathbf{Q}_i^{j-1}\|_2^2 \tag{6.6}$$

can be added to the objective function of Eq. 6.2. Typically, the weight λ_s, which accounts for the relative influence of the two terms, is set manually. In Torresani et al. [2008], a similar, though more general, linear dynamical model was introduced in a probabilistic framework. In that case, the temporal structure takes the form

$$\mathbf{c}^j = \Phi \mathbf{c}^{j-1} + \eta^j \,, \tag{6.7}$$

where $\mathbf{c}^j$ is the vector of all shape coefficients for frame j, Φ is an $N_s \times N_s$ transition matrix, and η^j is a zero-mean Gaussian noise vector. This model represents the shape coefficients in a frame as a linear function of those in the previous one. If Φ is taken to be the identity matrix, this essentially becomes equivalent to the previous zeroth order motion model.

For the same reasons that make it permissible to penalize large frame-to-frame shape variations, it can be assumed that the camera motion between two consecutive frames is small. In Rabaud and Belongie [2008, 2009], this was done by relying on the same zeroth order motion model as before and introducing the term

$$\lambda_r \sum_{j=2}^{N_f} \|\mathbf{R}^j - \mathbf{R}^{j-1}\|_F^2 \tag{6.8}$$

in the objective function of Eq. 6.2. As before, λ_r is the weight that controls the relative influence of the terms in the objective function. A similar regularizer can also be added for the translation when it is optimized.

In Olsen and Bartoli [2008], a single term was introduced to subsume both shape and camera temporal consistency regularizers by noting that their respective parameters appear simultaneously in $\mathbf{C}$. This yields a regularizer of the form

$$\lambda_m \sum_{j=2}^{N_f} \|\mathbf{C}_{2j-1:2j} - \mathbf{C}_{2j-3:2j-2}\|_F^2 \,, \tag{6.9}$$

where, as before, $\mathbf{C}_{2j-1:2j}$ is the $2 \times 3N_s$ matrix containing the two rows of $\mathbf{C}$ corresponding to frame j.

Recently, it was proposed to exploit a very different kind of temporal information Rabaud and Belongie [2008, 2009], Zhu et al. [2010]. Instead of assuming that frame-to-frame motion is small, these methods rely on the concept of repetitions and assume that, given a sufficiently long video sequence, similar shapes will appear several times, but seen from different viewpoints. Under this assumption, several frames picturing the same shape up to a rigid transformation can be used together to estimate the 3D shape.

In Rabaud and Belongie [2008], Zhu et al. [2010], the images were clustered based on a re-projection error criterion. Given a pair of images, epipolar geometry can be used to decide whether both images were generated by the same rigid object. Unfortunately, some cases remain ambiguous, and therefore triplets of images need to be compared. Once the image clusters in which the shape moves rigidly have been found, a standard rigid structure from motion technique, such as Tomasi and Kanade [1992], can be applied to reconstruct the shape in each cluster. To further improve the global reconstruction in the whole sequence, and account for temporally continuous deformations rather than piecewise rigid ones, an additional refinement step is performed. The major difference between Rabaud and Belongie [2008] and Zhu et al. [2010] arises from the fact that the former uses independent clusters of at least 3 frames, whereas the latter looks for as large as possible overlapping groups of images.

In Rabaud and Belongie [2009], a different method to account for these repetitions was proposed. Instead of using reprojection errors, a measure of similarity between triplets of shapes $\{\mathbf{Q}^i, \mathbf{Q}^j, \mathbf{Q}^k\}$ was introduced. It can be written as

$$a_F(i, j, k) = \sum_{h \in \{i,j,k\}} \left\| \mathbf{Q}^h - \frac{\mathbf{Q}^i + \mathbf{Q}^j + \mathbf{Q}^k}{3} \right\|_F^2 . \tag{6.10}$$

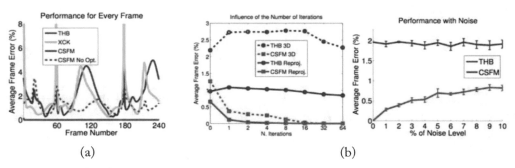

Figure 6.3: Comparison of the results of Rabaud and Belongie [2009](CSFM) with those of Xiao *et al.* [2004b](XCK) and Torresani *et al.* [2008](THB) on the shark data. (a) Reconstruction error for all frames in the sequence. (b) For a single frame, convergence speed and reconstruction error as a function of noise. Errors are given as mean distances between the reconstructed points and their true location, divided by the span of the true shape. Courtesy of V. Rabaud.

Of course, this measure cannot be directly computed, since it depends on the 3D shapes, which are unknown. However, its infimum and supremum can be obtained from the measurement matrix $\mathbf{W}$. This is used to build a set of pairs of triplets $\mathcal{F} = \{((i, j, k), (i', j', k'))|a_F(i, j, k) \leq a_F(i', j', k')\}$, which implicitly defines an ordering of triplets based on the similarity measure. Furthermore, it can be shown that a_F is related to the values of the shape coefficients, such that

$$a_F(i, j, k) = \frac{1}{3} \left(\|\mathbf{c}^i - \mathbf{c}^j\|_2^2 + \|\mathbf{c}^i - \mathbf{c}^k\|_2^2 + \|\mathbf{c}^j - \mathbf{c}^k\|_2^2 \right) . \tag{6.11}$$

Therefore, the relations in set $\mathcal{F}$ can be used to define constraints in a Generalized Non-metric Multi-Dimensional Scaling problem Agarwal *et al.* [2007] written as a semi-definite program (SDP). Solving this SDP yields an estimate of the shape coefficients $\mathbf{c}$ in each frame. Given the shape coefficients, the shape basis and rotations are then computed. Fig. 6.3 compares the reconstruction accuracy of Rabaud and Belongie [2009] with other methods on the shark dataset. The reconstruction errors are given as mean distances between the reconstructed points and their true location, divided by the span of the true shape. Note that the method of Rabaud and Belongie [2009] converges quickly and yields better accuracy than the other approaches.

While the zeroth order motion model and the shape repetition assumption are very helpful, they both have their shortcomings. The former usually does not really apply to the true dynamics of a deformable surface, and the latter requires having long enough sequences such that the same shape appears several times. Furthermore, in the above-mentioned works, temporal consistency was not sufficient to fully constrain reconstruction. As a consequence, the resulting techniques had to exploit additional geometric constraints, as described in Section 6.3.

6.2.1   FROM BASIS SHAPES TO BASIS TRAJECTORIES

As mentioned in Chapter 5, while most NRSFM approaches represent the shape with a linear subspace models, some recent works have proposed different formulations. Among them, the method of Akhter et al. [2008] introduced an alternative approach to enforcing temporal consistency by formulating NRSFM in trajectory space. In other words, instead of reconstructing the whole shape at each time instant, the trajectory over the whole sequence of each 3D point is estimated.

To this end, the usual shape basis is replaced by a trajectory basis, as shown in Fig. 6.4. More specifically, the $x-$, $y-$, and $z-$trajectories of a 3D point $\mathbf{q}_i = [x_i, y_i, z_i]^T$ in N_f frames are defined as $\mathbf{t}_i^x = [x_i^1, \cdots, x_i^{N_f}]^T$, $\mathbf{t}_i^y = [y_i^1, \cdots, y_i^{N_f}]^T$, and $\mathbf{t}_i^z = [z_i^1, \cdots, z_i^{N_f}]^T$, respectively. Assuming that these trajectories can be described as a linear combination of N_t basis trajectories θ_k, this yields

$$\mathbf{t}_i^x = \sum_{k=1}^{N_t} a_{i,k}^x \theta_k , \quad \mathbf{t}_i^y = \sum_{k=1}^{N_t} a_{i,k}^y \theta_k , \quad \mathbf{t}_i^z = \sum_{k=1}^{N_t} a_{i,k}^z \theta_k , \tag{6.12}$$

where $a_{i,k}^x$, $a_{i,k}^y$, and $a_{i,k}^z$ are the $x-$, $y-$, and $z-$coefficients for point i and basis trajectory k, and θ_k is an N_f-dimensional vector. Given this formulation, NRSFM can be re-written as the factorization problem

$$\mathbf{W} = \underbrace{\begin{bmatrix} \mathbf{R}^1 & & \\ & \cdots & \\ & & \mathbf{R}^{N_f} \end{bmatrix}}_{\Gamma} \underbrace{\begin{bmatrix} \beta^1 & & \\ & \beta^1 & \\ & & \beta^1 \\ \vdots & & \\ \beta^{N_f} & & \\ & \beta^{N_f} & \\ & & \beta^{N_f} \end{bmatrix}}_{} \underbrace{\begin{bmatrix} a_{1,1}^x & \cdots & a_{N_c,1}^x \\ \vdots & \vdots & \vdots \\ a_{1,N_t}^x & \cdots & a_{N_c,N_t}^x \\ a_{1,1}^y & \cdots & a_{N_c,1}^y \\ \vdots & \vdots & \vdots \\ a_{1,N_t}^y & \cdots & a_{N_c,N_t}^y \\ a_{1,1}^z & \cdots & a_{N_c,1}^z \\ \vdots & \vdots & \vdots \\ a_{1,N_t}^z & \cdots & a_{N_c,N_t}^z \end{bmatrix}}_{\Lambda} , \tag{6.13}$$

where $\beta^j = [\theta_1^j, \cdots, \theta_{N_t}^j]$ contains the jth element of all θ_k, and $\mathbf{W}$ is the same measurement matrix as before. $\mathbf{W}$ is then factorized into Γ and Λ, and the resulting corrective transform is estimated by ensuring that the rotation matrices are orthonormal. In practice, the Akhter et al. [2008] method assumes that the basis trajectories θ_k are known and can be generated from the Discrete Cosine Transform. While this might seem restrictive, it was shown to generalize to many different trajectories. The results are compared to those of Torresani et al. [2008] and Xiao et al. [2004b] in Fig. 6.5. Note that the reconstructions of Akhter et al. [2008] correspond more closely to what is depicted by the images.

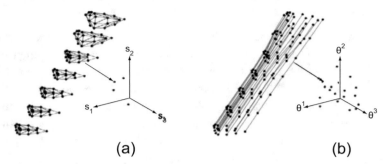

Figure 6.4: Comparison of shape and trajectory spaces. (a) In traditional approaches, a 3D object is represented as a point in shape space. (b) By contrast, in the approach of Akhter et al. [2008], the trajectory is represented by a single point in trajectory space. Courtesy of I. Akhter.

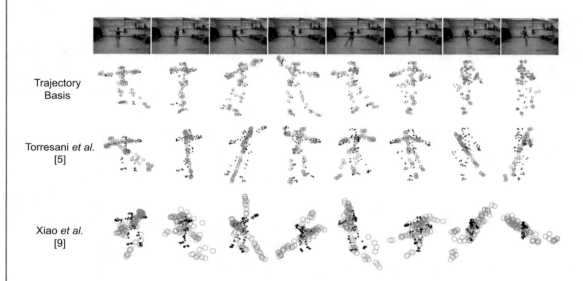

Figure 6.5: Comparison of several approaches on a dance sequence from the CMU mocap database. The images were based on Akhter et al. [2008]. Note that their method produces more accurate results than the others. Black dots represent the ground-truth points, whereas gray circles are the reconstructed ones. Courtesy of I. Akhter

In addition to its originality, this method has the advantage of only requiring orthonormality constraints as additional knowledge to yield accurate reconstruction. This is due to the fact that the basis is fixed, and therefore fewer unknowns need be determined in the reconstruction process.

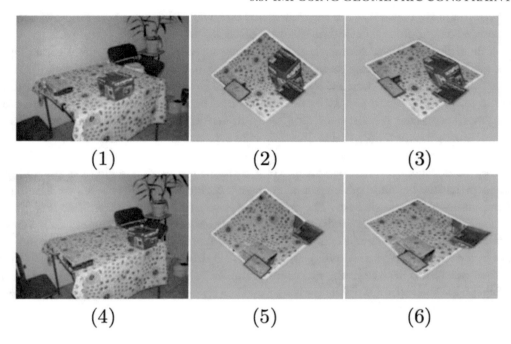

Figure 6.6: Comparison of the results of a weak perspective camera model Xiao *et al.* [2004b] and a full perspective one Xiao and Kanade [2005] when relying simultaneously on orthonormality constraints and basis constraints. (1,4) Two input images. (2,5) Reconstruction with a perspective model. (3,6) Reconstruction with a weak perspective model. Note that, in the latter case, some distortion can be observed. Courtesy of T. Kanade

6.3   IMPOSING GEOMETRIC CONSTRAINTS

While temporal consistency regularizers have proved effective in many situations, they still assume that the input images have been acquired in an orderly sequence and, therefore, do not generalize to cases where the images are independent. Furthermore, they are not always sufficient to fully disambiguate the reconstruction problem. As a consequence, many techniques have also exploited geometric properties for structure and motion estimation. Here, as in the template-based case, we distinguish between global and local shape constraints.

6.3.1   GLOBAL CONSTRAINTS

In contrast to the template-based approach presented in Chapter 3, the basic formulation of non-rigid structure from motion techniques introduced in Chapter 5 includes a global linear deformation model by design, since the surface is assumed to be generated from a linear combination of basis shapes. Note, however, that, in NRSFM, the basis shapes are unknown, and thus do not provide as strong constraints as they did in the template-based case, where they were pre-computed and fixed. This explains why additional smoothness constraints are often necessary in NRSFM.

One of the first global geometric constraints employed in NRSFM involved assuming that the mean shape is the dominant component of the shape in each frame. Constraining the surface reconstruction can then be done by encouraging the shape in each frame to remain close to the unknown mean shape Brand [2001], or close to an initial estimate computed using rigid structure from motion techniques Aanaes and Kahl [2002]. In essence, this assumption simply means that the object mostly moves rigidly, and is thus only valid for small deformations.

As mentioned in Section 5.4, recovering the basis shapes is an ambiguous problem, since there may be dependencies between them. As a consequence, there is a global affine ambiguity of the shape basis. Therefore, other types of geometric constraints were proposed to disambiguate the computation of the shape basis. The methods of Xiao and Kanade [2005], Xiao et al. [2004b] established basis constraints in a similar manner as the orthonormality constraints of Eqs. 6.4 and 6.5. To this end, they rely on the condition number of sub-matrices of $\mathbf{W}$ to find the most independent N_s images in the sequence. The corresponding, unknown 3D shapes are then taken as the basis shapes. Therefore, constraints arise from the fact that the surface in the chosen frames must be generated by a single basis shape. Ordering the frames so that the chosen ones are the first N_s frames in the sequence, this yields constraints of the form

$$
\begin{aligned}
c_i^i &= 1 , \; 1 \le i \le N_s , \\
c_i^j &= 0 , \; 1 \le i, j \le N_s , \; i \ne j .
\end{aligned}
\tag{6.14}
$$

Following the same approach as for the orthonormality constraints of Eqs. 6.4 and 6.5, these constraints can be used to derive linear equations in terms of the quadratic corrective transform $\mathbf{H}_k$. When used in conjunction with the orthonormality property, these constraints were shown to be sufficient to remove the ambiguity in NRSFM Xiao et al. [2004b]. In Fig. 6.6, we compare the results obtained with orthonormality constraints and basis constraints under a weak perspective model Xiao et al. [2004b] and a full perspective one Xiao and Kanade [2005]. Note that the weak perspective reconstruction is distorted.

A similar idea as in Xiao et al. [2004b] was proposed in Zhu et al. [2010]. The shape in a particular image is assumed to be generated by only a subset of all the basis shapes, and, therefore, the coefficients vectors $\mathbf{c}^j$ should be sparse. This is enforced by adding the penalty term

$$
\lambda_c \sum_{j=1}^{N_f} \| \mathbf{c}^j \|_1 ,
\tag{6.15}
$$

to the objective function, while imposing $\| \mathbf{c}^j \|_2^2 = 1 \; \forall j$. This proved effective to remove the rotation ambiguity of the shape basis.

Two other approaches have also been proposed to more directly encourage the basis shapes to remain independent. In Bartoli et al. [2008], a coarse-to-fine approach to recovering the modes was

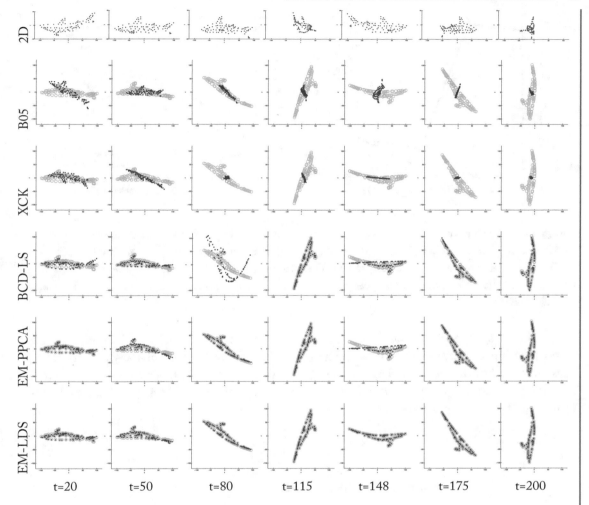

Figure 6.7: Comparison of the results of the various algorithms proposed in Torresani *et al.* [2008] (BCD-LS, EM-PPCA, EM-LDS), as well as of the methods in Xiao *et al.* [2004b] (XCK) and in Brand [2005] (B05) on the shark data. Green circles are the ground-truth points, and blue dots the reconstructed ones. Courtesy of A. Hertzmann. © 2008 IEEE.

introduced. It starts by computing the mean shape, and then iteratively adds modes to explain as much of the remaining variance of the data as possible. A stopping criterion based on cross-validation was defined to avoid overfitting to measurement noise. In Brandt *et al.* [2009], it was proposed to find independent basis shapes by following an ICA-based approach. To this end, a regularization term that minimizes the mutual information of the individual modes was introduced.

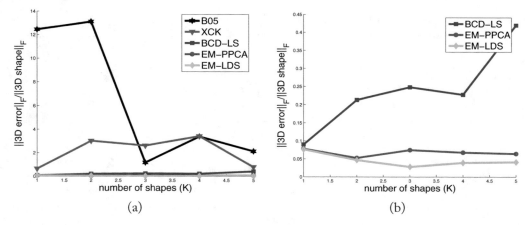

Figure 6.8: Evaluation of the robustness to the number of basis shapes on the shark data for the algorithms proposed in Torresani *et al.* [2008] (BCD-LS, EM-PPCA, EM-LDS) and the methods in Xiao *et al.* [2004b] (XCK) and in Brand [2005] (B05). The plot in (b) shows a zoomed version of the one in (a) to highlight the differences between the Torresani *et al.* [2008] algorithms. Courtesy of A. Hertzmann. © 2008 IEEE.

In the same spirit of constraining the reconstruction of the shape basis, the notion of shape priors was introduced in Del Bue [2008]. The general idea was to make use of known 3D shapes, and assume that they were generated by part of the same shape basis as the deformation observed in the input images. More specifically, let $\mathbf{L}$ be the $3l \times N_c$ matrix of known 3D shapes. The factorization problem of Eq. 6.1 can be re-written as

$$\mathbf{W} = [\mathbf{C}_J | \mathbf{C}_I] \begin{bmatrix} \mathbf{B}_J \\ \mathbf{B}_I \end{bmatrix} , \tag{6.16}$$

to which can be added constraints for the shape prior as

$$\mathbf{L} = \mathbf{N}\mathbf{B}_J , \tag{6.17}$$

where J is the set of indices of the basis shapes that are common to the prior shapes and the unknown ones, and I is the set containing the remaining indices. The factorization of both equations can then be done simultaneously via generalized singular value decomposition. The shapes given as prior were shown to significantly help reducing the ambiguities in the reconstructed shape basis, and, thus, in the overall factorization.

Instead of adding explicit constraints on the shape coefficients, in Torresani *et al.* [2008], it was proposed to replace the linear subspace model with probabilistic PCA (PPCA) Tipping and Bishop [1999], and to introduce a Gaussian prior on the coefficients. A benefit of using PPCA is that it makes it possible to marginalize out the shape coefficients. Therefore, the weights c_k^j are never

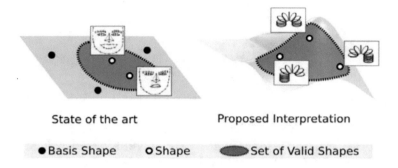

State of the art   Proposed Interpretation

● Basis Shape   ○ Shape   ⬮ Set of Valid Shapes

Figure 6.9: While standard NRSFM approaches assume that the shapes lie on a linear subspace, the true manifold can be nonlinear. This manifold can be better approximated by locally smooth manifold learning Rabaud and Belongie [2008]. Courtesy of V. Rabaud. © 2008 IEEE.

explicitly computed, which removes them from the variables to optimize. This is similar in spirit to the formulation of Section 4.2.2.2 for local deformation models, where the coefficients were directly obtained from the mesh vertices. By assuming Gaussian noise over the measurements and over the shape, the distribution over the measurements is also Gaussian. In this framework, NRSFM can be formulated as maximizing the joint likelihood of the image measurements whose negative logarithm can be written as

$$
\begin{aligned}
\mathcal{L} \;=\; & \frac{1}{2} \sum_{j=1}^{N_f} \left(\mathbf{w}^j - \mathbf{E}^j \bar{\mathbf{q}} \right)^T \left(\mathbf{E}^j \left(\mathbf{V}\mathbf{V}^T + \sigma_m^2 \mathbf{I} \right) \mathbf{E}^{j^T} + \sigma^2 \mathbf{I} \right) \left(\mathbf{w}^j - \mathbf{E}^j \bar{\mathbf{q}} \right) \\
+ \; & \frac{1}{2} \sum_{j=1}^{N_f} \ln \left| \mathbf{E}^j \left(\mathbf{V}\mathbf{V}^T + \sigma_m^2 \mathbf{I} \right) \mathbf{E}^{j^T} + \sigma^2 \mathbf{I} \right| + N_c N_f \ln(2\pi) \,,
\end{aligned}
\tag{6.18}
$$

where $\mathbf{w}^j$ is the vector containing the two rows of $\mathbf{W}$ associated to frame j, $\mathbf{E}^j$ replicates $d^j \mathbf{R}^j$ across the diagonal, with d^j the scalar accounting for depth in frame j, $\mathbf{V}$ is the matrix whose k^{th} column contains the vectorized basis shape $\mathbf{S}_k$, and $\bar{\mathbf{q}}$ contains the vectorized mean shape. σ_m and σ are the Gaussian noise variance of the shape and of the measurements, respectively. This negative log likelihood is minimized via an EM procedure, whose initialization is obtained using a rigid structure from motion technique. A comparison of the results of the different algorithms proposed in Torresani *et al.* [2008] and of other techniques on the shark data is shown in Fig. 6.7. Fig. 6.8 depicts the robustness to the number of basis shapes of the same algorithms. As before, the error is defined as the ratio between the 3D distance to ground-truth and the span of the true shape. Note that the error obtained by the EM procedure of Torresani *et al.* [2008] is relatively stable with respect to the number of basis shapes.

All the above-mentioned algorithms still rely on a linear subspace model to represent the deformations of the object of interest. In practice, this only applies to relatively simple deformations,

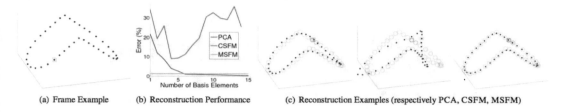

(a) Frame Example   (b) Reconstruction Performance   (c) Reconstruction Examples (respectively PCA, CSFM, MSFM)

Figure 6.10: Comparison of NRSFM using a locally smooth manifold representation of the shape space Rabaud and Belongie [2008] (MSFM) with a classical NRSFM method (CSFM) Torresani *et al.* [2008] and with PCA learned from known 3D shapes. Note that the method of Rabaud and Belongie [2008] is better adapted to cope with this non-smooth deformation of a circular shape. Courtesy of V. Rabaud. © 2008 IEEE.

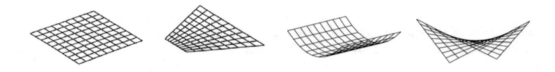

Figure 6.11: Quadratic deformation modes applied to a synthetic planar patch Fayad *et al.* [2009]. Courtesy of A. Del Bue.

especially since existing methods are only reliable when using a small number of basis shapes. Recently, two publications have advocated the use of alternative models to capture more complex deformations. The first one Rabaud and Belongie [2008] exploits the concept of locally smooth manifold learning (LSML) Dollar *et al.* [2007]. As suggested by Fig. 6.9, this relaxes the implicit constraint that the shapes lie on a linear subspace. Instead of optimizing basis shapes and their coefficients, the 3D coordinates of the object's points are optimized directly, and the resulting shapes are regularized to form a locally smooth manifold. This is done in an iterative manner. At each iteration, the manifold is learned from the current shape estimates. This yields a gradient for the LMSL error term, which is combined with a gradient computed from a temporal smoothness term explained in Section 6.2. As shown in Fig. 6.10, this approach has proved particularly well-adapted to model large deformations that do not lie on linear manifolds, and therefore cannot be captured by a linear subspace.

The second approach Fayad *et al.* [2009] to replacing the linear subspace model with a higher-order one exploits a quadratic deformation model, which was originally introduced in the Computer Graphics community for simulation purposes Müller *et al.* [2005]. In this case, the shape of a set of

BA-Quad

BA-Lin

EM-LDS

Figure 6.12: Comparison of the results obtained with global quadratic models Fayad *et al.* [2009], global linear models with bundle adjustment Del Bue *et al.* [2007] and the EM-LDS algorithm of Torresani *et al.* [2008]. Note that the quadratic models are better suited to model these large deformations. Courtesy of A. Del Bue.

points is expressed as

$$
\mathbf{Q} = \left[\ \Gamma \mid \Omega \mid \Lambda \ \right] \underbrace{\begin{bmatrix} x_1 & \cdots & x_{N_c} \\ y_1 & \cdots & y_{N_c} \\ z_1 & \cdots & z_{N_c} \\ \hline x_1^2 & \cdots & x_{N_c}^2 \\ y_1^2 & \cdots & y_{N_c}^2 \\ z_1^2 & \cdots & z_{N_c}^2 \\ \hline x_1 y_1 & \cdots & x_{N_c} y_{N_c} \\ y_1 z_1 & \cdots & y_{N_c} z_{N_c} \\ z_1 x_1 & \cdots & z_{N_c} x_{N_c} \end{bmatrix}}_{\hat{\mathbf{Q}}} , \qquad (6.19)
$$

where Γ, Ω, and Λ are 3×3 matrices containing the coefficients of the linear, quadratic, and mixed terms, respectively. This formulation relies on the availability of a rest shape $\hat{\mathbf{Q}}$ that can be obtained from a rigid factorization algorithm. One advantage of this shape parameterization is that the basis is completely determined by the rest shape. Therefore, there is no need to optimize it. Some of the corresponding basis shapes are depicted in Fig. 6.11. One drawback of this model is that, if the values of the coefficients are left unconstrained, it can produce unrealistic shapes. On the other hand, when the coefficients are initialized correctly and are appropriately bounded, the resulting technique allows for the reconstruction of complex shapes, as depicted by Fig. 6.12.

6.3.2   LOCAL CONSTRAINTS

As for template-based reconstruction, while global geometric constraints are mostly effective to reconstruct simple global deformations, local approaches are in general better suited to account for complex deformations. This is still the case when compared to the quadratic models, which, as depicted in Fig. 6.11, produce deformation modes similar to those of the learned linear models of Section 4.2.2.1, but without requiring training data. In this section, we present several approaches to incorporating local smoothness in NRSFM. While some of them are introduced to replace the linear subspace model, others are used in conjunction with it: Since the shape basis is learned during reconstruction, which is underconstrained, it can still be improved by imposing additional smoothness.

The first local smoothness term in NRSFM was introduced in Torresani *et al.* [2001]. As in the original Snakes Kass *et al.* [1988], the local constraints are encoded as a regularizer on neighboring points. More specifically, for neighboring points $\mathbf{q}_{i_1}$ and $\mathbf{q}_{i_2}$, the regularization term is written as

$$\alpha_{i_1,i_2}^2 \sum_{k=1}^{N_s} (\mathbf{S}_{k,i_1} - \mathbf{S}_{k,i_2})^2 \; , \tag{6.20}$$

where $\mathbf{S}_{k,i}$ contains the 3D coordinates corresponding to point i in basis $\mathbf{S}_k$. The neighborhood can be established by nearest neighbor search or Delaunay triangulation in image space. The weights α_{i_1,i_2} are taken to be inversely proportional to the 2D distance between points i_1 and i_2.

In Olsen and Bartoli [2008], a similar idea was proposed, but with an additional temporal component. The regularizer exploits the fact that the tracks of two simultaneously visible points should have similar shapes. This can be written as

$$\alpha_{i_1,i_2} \left\| \mathbf{q}_{i_1}^J - \mathbf{q}_{i_2}^J \right\|_2^2 \; , \tag{6.21}$$

where $\mathbf{q}_i^J$ is the vector concatenating the 3D coordinates of point i in the set of frames J. As before, the weights α_{i_1,i_2} are taken as inversely proportional to the 2D distance between the points. These constraints are included for all pairs of points that have been tracked simultaneously for at least 10 frames.

Another approach to incorporating local constraints into NRSFM is to assume local rigidity of the deforming surface. In Llado *et al.* [2010], it was assumed that, while some points on the surface deform, others only move rigidly throughout the sequence. The problem then becomes one of distinguishing rigid from non-rigid motion, which can be done automatically Llado *et al.* [2010]. As the methods relying on shape repetitions Rabaud and Belongie [2008], Zhu *et al.* [2010] introduced in Section 6.2, this involves verifying how well points satisfy epipolar geometry. Since many points also move non-rigidly, and therefore should be considered as outliers in the fundamental matrices computation, a RANSAC algorithm is employed. Furthermore, to speedup this procedure, a degree of non-rigidity score is defined and used to build a prior to guide the RANSAC algorithm.

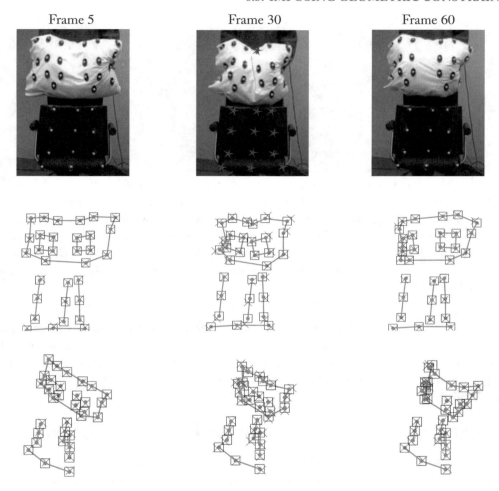

Figure 6.13: Reconstruction of a deforming cushion Llado *et al.* [2010]. The approach relies on the rigid chair to constrain the motion estimation. On the second and third rows, the reconstructed surface is shown from two different viewpoints. Courtesy of A. Del Bue.

The segmented rigid points are then used to compute the motion parameters. Finally, the non-rigid structure is estimated via a nonlinear optimization procedure. In this case, the surface is still computed as a linear combination of basis shapes. This assumption of rigidly moving points proved valid for face reconstruction, or when several objects are moving with respect to each other, as shown in Fig. 6.13. However, this does not generalize to arbitrary non-rigid objects.

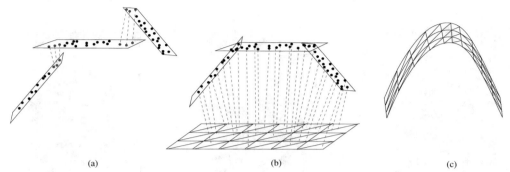

(a)   (b)   (c)

Figure 6.14: Modeling the surface as a consistent collection of planar patches Varol *et al.* [2009]. **(a)** Image patches are reconstructed individually up to a scale ambiguity which causes their reconstructions not to be aligned. **(b)** Using shared correspondences between these patches (blue points), consistent scales for all patches are recovered and the whole surface is reconstructed up to a single global scale. **(c)** Optionally, a triangulated mesh is fitted to the resulting 3D point cloud to account for holes and outliers. It can be used to provide a common surface representation across the frames and to enforce temporal consistency. © 2009 IEEE.

While geometric constraints have proved effective at disambiguating reconstruction, all the methods described above still treat the object of interest as a whole. As a consequence, similarly as the global models of Chapter 4, they often are limited to relatively simple deformations. In the next section, we present approaches that address this shortcoming by separating the object of interest into local regions.

6.4   SPLITTING A GLOBAL SURFACE INTO LOCAL ONES

As discussed in Section 4.2.2.1, even when the global deformations are large, purely local ones tend to be smaller and easier to recover. Therefore, it has recently been proposed to also perform NRSFM locally, so that more complex deformations can be handled. As we will see, local deformations can often be modeled as planar Varol *et al.* [2009], quadratic Fayad *et al.* [2010], or isometric Taylor *et al.* [2010]. In essence, these approaches therefore perform NRSFM to recover local surface patches and then enforce consistency between these patches to build a global surface. These methods have significanlty departed from the formulation presented in Chapter 5.

The method introduced in Varol *et al.* [2009] and depicted by Fig. 6.14 relies on the fact that, when the global deformations are not too severe, local surface patches remain approximately planar. It takes advantage of the fact that the motion of a plane from one image to the next can be represented as a homography Hartley and Zisserman [2000]. Given corresponding points in an image pair, the first image is subdivided into overlapping patches such as those of Fig. 6.14(a), which are assumed to remain roughly planar. Within each individual patch, the correspondences are used to compute a homography that relates its appearance in the first image to that in the second one. From

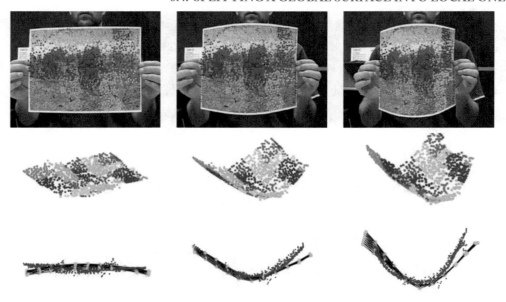

Figure 6.15: Using local quadratic models Fayad *et al.* [2010]. Top and middle rows: Reconstruction results on a real sequence. Bottom row: Comparison with the reconstructions of Varol *et al.* [2009], depicted by a mesh with green vertices. Note that the Fayad *et al.* [2010] reconstruction is more accurate both because it was obtained from a whole video sequences and because it allows for deformations of the patches. Courtesy of A. Del Bue.

this homography, the rotation, translation and patch normal can be computed up to a global scale ambiguity and a twofold normal ambiguity Malis and Vargas [2007], Zhang and Hanson [1995]. In other words, each 2D point in a patch can be assigned one of several 3D interpretations. These ambiguities are resolved by using points that belong to multiple patches, such as those shown in blue in Fig. 6.14(a), to enforce consistency. This is done by guaranteeing that they receive the *same* interpretation, no matter what patch is used to reconstruct them. First, normal orientations are chosen consistently across patches. Then, the scale of each patch is optimized such that the distance between the 3D reconstruction of the same 2D point from different patches is minimized. One strength of this approach is that each step only involves solving a linear system, which can be done in closed-form. Furthermore, as opposed to classical NRSFM techniques, this method allows reconstruction from only two images depicting two different shapes of the same surface.

One drawback of the Varol *et al.* [2009] method is that it requires sufficiently many corre-spondences per local patch to reliably estimate the homography. As a consequence, relatively large portions of the surface are asssumed to be planar, which limits the range of global deformation.

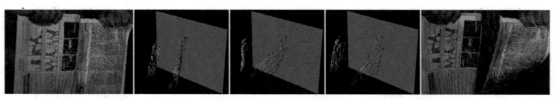

Figure 6.16: Reconstruction of a piece of paper being torn apart Taylor *et al.* [2010]. Courtesy of A. Jepson. © 2010 IEEE.

In Fayad *et al.* [2010], the authors extended this approach to allow for more complex deformations of the individual patches, given 2D points tracked across a video sequence. Instead of imposing local planarity, local deformation are regularized using the quadratic deformation model discussed in Section 6.3.1 Fayad *et al.* [2009]. Each overlapping group of tracked 2D points is reconstructed independently using the quadratic deformation model of Eq. 6.19. As in the global case, this requires a rest shape, which can be obtained from the first few initial frames of the sequence using a rigid structure-from-motion technique. As in Varol *et al.* [2009], the scale ambiguity of each patch, is resolved by exploiting the overlap between the patches. The top two rows of Fig. 6.15 depict results obtained on real images of a piece of paper undergoing large deformations. The bottom row features a comparison of this approach with Varol *et al.* [2009]. Note that the reconstructions of Fayad *et al.* [2009] are more accurate than those of Varol *et al.* [2009]. This seems reasonable both because the method of Fayad *et al.* [2009] exploits the whole sequence instead of just two images, and because allowing the patches to deform is a better approximation of the observed phenomenon.

The two methods described above implicitly assume some amount of smoothness in the local deformations. By contrast, the method of Taylor *et al.* [2010] relies exclusively on the preservation of local Euclidean distances between feature points found on the surface, much as the Ecker *et al.* [2008], Perriollat *et al.* [2010] methods introduced in Section 4.2.2.1. Note, however, that in the NRSFM framework, the true distances between pairs of points are unknown. To overcome this problem, triplets of neighboring points that move rigidly are identified and the global shape reconstructed as a soup of triangles whose vertices remain at a fixed distance from each other. More specifically, under orthographic projection, the 3D length of an edge between points $\mathbf{q}_{i_1}$ and $\mathbf{q}_{i_2}$ is related to the length of its projection in the image plane by

$$\|\mathbf{q}_{i_1} - \mathbf{q}_{i_2}\|_2^2 - \|\mathbf{p}_{i_1} - \mathbf{p}_{i_2}\|_2^2 = (d_{i_1} - d_{i_2})^2 \,, \tag{6.22}$$

where $\mathbf{p}_i$ is the 2D projection of point i, and d_i is its depth. Furthermore, the sum of pairwise depth differences within a single triangle is always equal to zero, which can be written as

$$(d_2 - d_1) + (d_3 - d_2) + (d_1 - d_3) = 0 \,. \tag{6.23}$$

Combining these two equations for a single triangle moving rigidly in N_f frames results in the system of equations

$$\mathbf{d}^T \Lambda \mathbf{d} - 2\mathbf{d}^T \Lambda \mathbf{1}^1 + \mathbf{1}^{1^T} \Lambda \mathbf{1}^1 = 0$$
$$\vdots$$
$$\mathbf{d}^T \Lambda \mathbf{d} - 2\mathbf{d}^T \Lambda \mathbf{1}^{N_f} + \mathbf{1}^{N_f^T} \Lambda \mathbf{1}^{N_f} = 0 , \tag{6.24}$$

where

$$\mathbf{d} = \begin{bmatrix} \|\mathbf{q}_2 - \mathbf{q}_1\|_2^2 \\ \|\mathbf{q}_3 - \mathbf{q}_2\|_2^2 \\ \|\mathbf{q}_1 - \mathbf{q}_3\|_2^2 \end{bmatrix} , \ \mathbf{1}^j = \begin{bmatrix} \|\mathbf{p}_2^j - \mathbf{p}_1^j\|_2^2 \\ \|\mathbf{p}_3^j - \mathbf{p}_2^j\|_2^2 \\ \|\mathbf{p}_1^j - \mathbf{p}_3^j\|_2^2 \end{bmatrix} , \ \Lambda = \begin{bmatrix} 1 & -1 & -1 \\ -1 & 1 & -1 \\ -1 & -1 & 1 \end{bmatrix} . \tag{6.25}$$

Since the quadratic term in $\mathbf{d}$ is the same in all the equations, it can easily be eliminated. This yields a linear system of equations in $\mathbf{d}$, which can be solved in closed-form. From $\mathbf{d}$, the 3D triangle can be reconstructed up to a depth sign flip and a global depth ambiguity. These ambiguities are then solved by accounting for all rigidly moving triangles in the images. The non-rigid triangles are discarded based on their reprojection error. A strength of this approach is that it can handle topology changes, as when the sheet of paper depicted by Fig. 6.16 is being torn in two. A potential limitation that it shares with the Ecker et al. [2008], Perriollat et al. [2010], Salzmann et al. [2008a] methods discussed in Section 4.2.2.1, which also rely on 3D distance constraints, is that the Euclidean distances between triplets of surface points does not truly remain constant when the surface deforms. The approximation is only valid when the curvature of the triangle linking them is small, which means that the points cannot be too distant from each other.

In short, there has been a number of exciting recent advances in NRSFM that are now departing from its early formulations Bregler et al. [2000], Ullman [1983]. These new techniques are starting to produce results and appear to be more robust to noise and able to handle much larger deformations than before. This indicates that reliable solutions to this problem might be found in spite of its complexity.

CHAPTER 7

Future Directions

In this survey, we have reviewed several template-based and non-rigid structure-from-motion techniques that can be used to robustly recover 3D shape given point correspondences. The former can be made very reliable when a template is available but are of course inappropriate otherwise, which is often the case in practice. When video sequences are available, the latter can be invoked instead and are very effective when the deformations are not too complex.

In both cases, shape recovery implies solving an ill-posed problem and additional geometric or temporal consistency constraints are needed for good results. Furthermore, when there are too few correspondences, for example because the surfaces are relatively featureless, neither class of techniques performs well, which greatly limits their applicability. To remedy this situation, we believe that future research should focus on taking advantage of additional sources of image information, such as

- **Silhouettes:** The projected contours of a surface give powerful clues as to their 3D shape. They already have been extensively exploited to reconstruct developable surfaces Gumerov et al. [2004], Perriollat and Bartoli [2007], as discussed in Chapter 4. However, these approaches do not naturally generalize to non-developable surfaces whose shape cannot be inferred from their outlines, which often are occluding contours. Such contours have been used for 3D surface reconstruction Ilić et al. [2007], Sullivan et al. [1994], Szeliski and Weiss [1998] but most existing approaches rely on iterative schemes in which the occluding contours are predicted from a current shape estimate and compared to their observed image locations. This runs contrary to the spirit of the most effective template-based method that perform reconstruction either in closed form or by finding the minimum of a convex function. Further work is therefore required to merge these two different strands of research.

- **Texture:** Inferring shape from correspondences requires texture, since the correspondences typically only are established between interest points. However, this only uses a fraction of the available information; The orientation of the patches surrounding the interest points can also be inferred from textural deformations Hinterstoisser et al. [2011]. In other words, when correspondences can be established, it is usually also possible to estimate the surface normals. In Moreno-Noguer et al. [2009], such estimates were used to relax the inextensibility constraints required by an earlier template-based method Salzmann et al. [2008a], while still computing the 3D shape in closed-form. Other approaches discussed in this survey could and should be similarly extended to make the most of the texture, especially when the surface is not uniformly well-textured.

- **Shading:** It has long been known as a useful but fragile source of shape information Horn and Brooks [1989], which naturally complements textural cues where the albedos are constant or vary slowly Fua and Leclerc [1995]. As discussed in Chapter 4, it was used in White and Forsyth [2006] to disambiguate the direction of normals obtained from textural clues, in Moreno-Noguer *et al.* [2009] to provide normal estimates around interest points, and in Moreno-Noguer *et al.* [2010] to choose among competing shapes that all result in roughly the same image projections. The shading models used by these algorithms, however, remain simplistic. They would need to be extended further to prove truly useful outside of very specialized applications, such as virtually flattening a book to produce better photocopies Zhang *et al.* [2004]. We believe that a promising direction is to use modern statistical learning techniques to relate gray level patterns within image patches to local 3D shape estimates using realistic training data and without making unwarranted assumptions.

In addition to means of exploiting the image data more thoroughly, better and more widely applicable deformation models are required to break the ambiguities that plague monocular 3D surface reconstruction. When the surface is made of a material that is known *a priori*, effective models can be learned offline using training data. In the more general case when the surface material is not known beforehand, the model could be learned online using the parts of the surface that are sufficiently well-textured for a very simple regularizing prior to be enough to obtain valid reconstructions. This model could then be used to constrain the reconstruction of the rest of the surface. For similar purposes, one could also exploit transfer learning techniques that leverage labeled data of related problems to learn a model for a different problem where no, or very few, labeled data is available. In our context, given the training examples for some materials, we could learn a deformation model for a new material from very small amounts of reconstructed 3D shapes.

In short, current monocular approaches to 3D surface reconstruction can be well formalized and already yield promising results on well-textured surfaces. Much work is still required to make them fully operational on less well-textured surfaces but the way forward seems relatively clear.

Bibliography

H. Aanaes and F. Kahl. Estimation of Deformable Structure and Motion. In *Vision and Modelling of Dynamic Scenes Workshop*, 2002. 53, 56, 62, 68

S. Agarwal, J. Wills, L. Cayton, G. Lanckriet, D. Kriegman, and S. Belongie. Generalized Non-Metric Multidimensional Scaling. In *International Conference on Artificial Intelligence and Statistics*, 2007. 64

A. Ahmed and A. Farag. A New Formulation for Shape from Shading for Non-Lambertian Surfaces. In *Conference on Computer Vision and Pattern Recognition*, June 2006. DOI: 10.1109/CVPR.2006.35 18

I. Akhter, Y. Sheikh, S. Khan, and T. Kanade. Nonrigid Structure from Motion in Trajectory Space. In *Neural Information Processing Systems*, December 2008. 65, 66

I. Akhter, Y. Sheikh, and S. Khan. In Defense of Orthonormality Constraints for Nonrigid Structure from Motion. In *Conference on Computer Vision and Pattern Recognition*, June 2009. DOI: 10.1109/CVPR.2009.5206620 56, 60, 61

P. Baerlocher and R. Boulic. An Inverse Kinematics Architecture for Enforcing an Arbitrary Number of Strict Priority Levels. *The Visual Computer*, 2004. DOI: 10.1007/s00371-004-0244-4 47

D. Baraff and A. Witkin. Large Steps in Cloth Simulation. In *ACM SIGGRAPH*, pages 43–54, 1998. DOI: 10.1145/280814.280821 7

J. Barbič and D.L. James. Real-Time Subspace Integration for St. Venant-Kirchhoff Deformable Models. *ACM SIGGRAPH*, 24(3):982–990, August 2005. DOI: 10.1145/1073204.1073300 7

A. Bartoli and A. Zisserman. Direct Estimation of Non-Rigid Registration. In *British Machine Vision Conference*, September 2004. 19

A. Bartoli, V. Gay-Bellile, U. Castellani, J. Peyras, S. Olsen, and P. Sayd. Coarse-to-Fine Low-Rank Structure-from-Motion. In *Conference on Computer Vision and Pattern Recognition*, 2008. DOI: 10.1109/CVPR.2008.4587694 54, 57, 68

K.-J. Bathe. *Finite Element Procedures in Engineering Analysis*. Prentice Hall, 1982. 5, 6

M. Belkin and P. Niyogi. Laplacian Eigenmaps and Spectral Techniques for Embedding and Clustering. In *Neural Information Processing Systems*, pages 585–591. MIT Press, 2001. 10

K. S. Bhat, C. D. Twigg, J. K. Hodgins, P. K. Khosla, Z. Popovic, and S. M. Seitz. Estimating Cloth Simulation Parameters from Video. In *ACM Symposium on Computer Animation*, 2003. 2, 8

V. Blanz and T. Vetter. A Morphable Model for the Synthesis of 3D Faces. In *ACM SIGGRAPH*, pages 187–194, August 1999. DOI: 10.1145/311535.311556 12, 13, 39, 40

V. Blanz, C. Basso, T. Poggio, and T. Vetter. Reanimating Faces in Images and Video. In *Eurographics*, September 2003. 12

F.L. Bookstein.   Principal warps: Thin-plate splines and the decomposition of deformations.   *IEEE Transactions on Pattern Analysis and Machine Intelligence*, 11(6):567–585, 1989. DOI: 10.1109/34.24792 19

M. Botsch, M. Pauly, M. Wicke, and M. Gross. Adaptive Space Deformations Based on Rigid Cells. In *Eurographics*, 2007. DOI: 10.1111/j.1467-8659.2007.01056.x 7

S. Boyd and L. Vandenberghe. *Convex Optimization*. Cambridge University Press, 2004. 31, 46

D. Bradley, T. Popa, A. Sheffer, W. Heidrich, and T. Boubekeur. Markerless Garment Capture. *ACM Trans. Graph.*, 27(3), 2008. DOI: 10.1145/1360612.1360698 2

M. Brand.   Morphable 3D Models from Video. *Journal of Machine Learning Research*, 2001. DOI: 10.1109/CVPR.2001.990997 57, 68

M. Brand. A Direct Method of 3D Factorization of Nonrigid Motion Observed in 2D. In *Conference on Computer Vision and Pattern Recognition*, pages 122–128, 2005. DOI: 10.1109/CVPR.2005.23 60, 61, 69, 70

S.S. Brandt, P. Koskenkorva, J. Kannala, and A. Heyden. Uncalibrated non-rigid factorisation with automatic shape basis selection. In *Second Workshop on Non-Rigid Shape Analysis and Deformable Image Alignment (NORDIA'09)*, 2009. DOI: 10.1109/ICCVW.2009.5457678 69

C. Bregler, A. Hertzmann, and H. Biermann.   Recovering Non-Rigid 3D Shape from Image Streams.   In *Conference on Computer Vision and Pattern Recognition*, 2000. DOI: 10.1109/CVPR.2000.854941 51, 52, 60, 61, 79

R. Bridson, R. Fedkiw, and J. Anderson.   Robust Treatment of Collisions, Contact and Friction for Cloth Animation.   In *ACM Transactions on Graphics*, pages 594–603, 2002. DOI: 10.1145/1198555.1198572 7

R. Bridson, S. Marino, and R. Fedkiw. Simulation of Clothing With Folds and Wrinkles. In *ACM Symposium on Computer Animation*, 2003. 7

F. Brunet, R. Hartley, A. Bartoli, N. Navab, and R. Malgouyres. Monocular Template-based Reconstruction of Smooth and Inextensible Surfaces. In *Asian Conference on Computer Vision*, 2010. DOI: 10.1007/s11263-010-0352-8 40

J.C. Carr, Richard R.K. Beatson, J.B. Cherrie, T.J. Mitchell, W. Richard Fright, B.C. McCallum, and T.R. Evans. Reconstruction and Representation of 3D Objects With Radial Basis Functions. In *ACM SIGGRAPH*, 2001. DOI: 10.1145/383259.383266 14

E. Catmull and J. Clark. Recursively Generated B-Spline Surfaces on Arbitrary Topological Meshes. *Computer Aided Design Journal*, 10:350–355, 1978. DOI: 10.1016/0010-4485(78)90110-0 7, 14

F. Cirak, M. Ortiz, and P. Schröder. Subdivision Surfaces: a New Paradigm for Thin-Shell Finite-Element Analysis. *International Journal for Numerical Methods in Engineering*, 47:2039–2072, 2000.
DOI: 10.1002/(SICI)1097-0207(20000430)47:12%3C2039::AID-NME872%3E3.0.CO;2-1 7

L.D. Cohen and I. Cohen. Finite-Element Methods for Active Contour Models and Balloons for 2D and 3D Images. *IEEE Transactions on Pattern Analysis and Machine Intelligence*, 15(11):1131–1147, November 1993. DOI: 10.1109/34.244675 8, 45

P. Comon. Independent Component Analysis, a New Concept? *Journal of Machine Learning Research*, 36(3):287–314, 1994. DOI: 10.1016/0165-1684(94)90029-9 10

T. F. Cootes and C. J. Taylor. Active Shape Models - 'smart Snakes. In *British Machine Vision Conference*, pages 266–275, 1992. 11

T.F. Cootes, G.J. Edwards, and C.J. Taylor. Active Appearance Models. In *European Conference on Computer Vision*, pages 484–498, June 1998. 11

S. Coquillart. Extended Free-Form Deformation: a Sculpturing Tool for 3D Geometric Modeling. *ACM SIGGRAPH*, 24(4):187–196, 1990. DOI: 10.1145/97880.97900 14

D.P. Cosker, A.D. Marshall, P.L. Rosin, and Y.A. Hicks. Speech-driven facial animation using a hierarchical model. *Vision, Image and Signal Processing*, 151(4):314–321, 2004. DOI: 10.1049/ip-vis:20040752 12

N. Courtois, A. Klimov, J. Patarin, and A. Shamir. Efficient Algorithms for Solving Overdefined Systems of Multivariate Polynomial Equations. In *EUROCRYPT*, 2000. 38, 44

E. de Aguiar, C. Theobalt, C. Stoll, and H.-H. Seidel. Marker-Less Deformable Mesh Tracking for Human Shape and Motion Capture. In *Conference on Computer Vision and Pattern Recognition*, June 2007. DOI: 10.1109/CVPR.2007.383296 2

A. Del Bue, F. Smeraldi, and L. Agapito. Non-Rigid-Structure from Motion Using Ranklet-Based Tracking and Non-Linear Optimization. *Image Vision Computing*, 25:297–310, March 2007. DOI: 10.1016/j.imavis.2005.10.004 62, 73

A. Del Bue, J. Xavier, L. Agapito, and M. Paladini. Bilinear Factorization via Augmented Lagrange Multipliers. In *European Conference on Computer Vision*, 2010. DOI: 10.1007/978-3-642-15561-1_21 58

A. Del Bue. A Factorization Approach to Structure from Motion With Shape Priors. In *Conference on Computer Vision and Pattern Recognition*, June 2008. DOI: 10.1109/CVPR.2008.4587708 70

H. Delingette, M. Hebert, and K. Ikeuchi. Deformable Surfaces: A Free-Form Shape Representation. In *SPIE Geometric Methods in Computer Vision*, pages 21–30, 1991. DOI: 10.1117/12.49972 14

M. Dimitrijević, S. Ilić, and P. Fua. Accurate Face Models from Uncalibrated and Ill-Lit Video Sequences. In *Conference on Computer Vision and Pattern Recognition*, June 2004. DOI: 10.1109/CVPR.2004.26 12

P. Dollar, V. Rabaud, and S. Belongie. Non-Isometric Manifold Learning: Analysis and an Algorithm. In *International Conference in Machine Learning*, 2007. DOI: 10.1145/1273496.1273527 72

D. Doo and M. Sabin. Behaviour of Recursive Division Surfaces Near Extraordinary Points. *Computer Aided Design Journal*, 10(6):356–360, 1978. DOI: 10.1016/0010-4485(78)90111-2 7, 14

N. Dyn, David Levine, and John A. Gregory. A Butterfly Subdivision Scheme for Surface Interpolation With Tension Control. *ACM Transactions on Graphics*, 9(2):160–169, April 1990. DOI: 10.1145/78956.78958 14

M. Eck and H. Hoppe. Automatic Reconstruction of B-Spline Surfaces of Arbitrary Topological Type. In *ACM SIGGRAPH*, pages 325–334, 1996. DOI: 10.1145/237170.237271 14

A. Ecker, A.D. Jepson, and K.N. Kutulakos. Semidefinite Programming Heuristics for Surface Reconstruction Ambiguities. In *European Conference on Computer Vision*, October 2008. DOI: 10.1007/978-3-540-88682-2_11 44, 45, 78, 79

P. Faloutsos, M. van de Panne, and D. Terzopoulos. Dynamic Free-Form Deformations for Animation Synthesis. *IEEE Transactions on Visualization and Computer Graphics*, 1997. DOI: 10.1109/2945.620488 14

J. Fayad, A. Del Bue, L. Agapito, and P. M. Q. Aguiar. Non-Rigid Structure from Motion Using Quadratic Deformation Models. In *British Machine Vision Conference*, 2009. 72, 73, 78

J. Fayad, L. Agapito, and A. Del Bue. Piecewise Quadratic Reconstruction of Non-Rigid Surfaces from Monocular Sequences. In *European Conference on Computer Vision*, 2010. 76, 77, 78

G.D. Finlayson, S.D. Hordley, C. Lu, and M.S. Drew. On the removal of shadows from images. *IEEE Transactions on Pattern Analysis and Machine Intelligence*, 28(1):59–68, 2006. DOI: 10.1109/TPAMI.2006.18 12

M.A Fischler and R.C. Bolles. Random Sample Consensus: A Paradigm for Model Fitting With Applications to Image Analysis and Automated Cartography. *Communications ACM*, 24(6):381–395, 1981. DOI: 10.1145/358669.358692 58

D.A. Forsyth and A. Zisserman. Reflections on Shading. *IEEE Transactions on Pattern Analysis and Machine Intelligence*, 13(7):671–679, July 1991. DOI: 10.1109/34.85657 18

P. Fua and Y. G. Leclerc. Object-Centered Surface Reconstruction: Combining Multi-Image Stereo and Shading. *International Journal of Computer Vision*, 16:35–56, September 1995. DOI: 10.1007/BF01428192 8, 49, 82

P. Fua. Model-Based Optimization: Accurate and Consistent Site Modeling. In *International Society for Photogrammetry and Remote Sensing*, July 1996. 5

M.A. Greminger and B.J. Nelson. Deformable Object Tracking Using the Boundary Element Method. In *Conference on Computer Vision and Pattern Recognition*, 2003. DOI: 10.1109/CVPR.2003.1211366 8

M.A. Greminger and B.J. Nelson. A Deformable Object Tracking Algorithm Based on the Boundary Element Method That Is Robust to Occlusions and Spurious Edges. *International Journal of Computer Vision*, 78(1):29–45, 2008. DOI: 10.1007/s11263-007-0076-6 8

E. Grinspun, Anil N. Hirani, Mathieu Desbrun, and Peter Schröder. Discrete Shells. In *ACM Symposium on Computer Animation*, pages 62–67, 2003. 7

N.A. Gumerov, A. Zandifar, R. Duraiswami, and L.S. Davis. Structure of Applicable Surfaces from Single Views. In *European Conference on Computer Vision*, May 2004. DOI: 10.1007/978-3-540-24672-5_38 33, 81

C.G. Harris and M.J. Stephens. A Combined Corner and Edge Detector. In *Fourth Alvey Vision Conference*, 1988. 19

R. Hartley and F. Schaffalitzky. Reconstruction from Projections Using Grassmann Tensors. In *European Conference on Computer Vision*, pages 363–375, 2004. DOI: 10.1007/s11263-009-0225-1 56

R. Hartley and R. Vidal. Perspective Nonrigid Shape and Motion Recovery. In *European Conference on Computer Vision*, October 2008. DOI: 10.1007/978-3-540-88682-2_22 52, 54, 55, 56, 57

R. Hartley and A. Zisserman. *Multiple View Geometry in Computer Vision*. Cambridge University Press, 2000. 29, 76

M. Hauth and W. Strasser. Corotational Simulation of Deformable Solids. In *International Conference in Central Europe on Computer Graphics, Visualization and Computer Vision*, pages 137–145, 2004. 7

C. Hernandez, G. Vogiatzis, G. J. Brostow, B. Stenger, and R. Cipolla. Non-Rigid Photometric Stereo With Colored Lights. In *International Conference on Computer Vision*, October 2007. DOI: 10.1109/ICCV.2007.4408939 3

A. Hertzmann and S. M. Seitz. Shape and Materials by Example: A Photometric Stereo Approach. In *Conference on Computer Vision and Pattern Recognition*, pages 533–540, 2003. DOI: 10.1109/CVPR.2003.1211400 3

S. Hinterstoisser, S. Ilic, N. Navab, P. Fua, and V. Lepetit. Learning Real-Time Perspective Patch Rectification. *International Journal of Computer Vision*, 2011. Accepted for publication. DOI: 10.1007/s11263-010-0379-x 81

G. Hirota, S. Fisher, and M. Lin. Simulation of Non-Penetrating Elastic Bodies Using Distance Fields. Technical report, University of North Carolina, 2000. 7

H. Hoppe, T. Derose, T. Duchamp, M. Halstead, H. Jun, J. Mcdonald, J. Schweitzer, and W. Stuetzle. Piecewise Smooth Surface Reconstruction. In *ACM SIGGRAPH*, pages 295–302, 1994. DOI: 10.1145/192161.192233 14

B.K.P. Horn and M.J. Brooks. *Shape from Shading*. MIT Press, 1989. 18, 82

D. H. House and David E. Breen, editors. *Cloth Modeling and Animation*. A. K. Peters, Ltd., 2000. 7

W.C. Huang, D.B. Goldgof, and L.V. Tsap. Nonlinear Finite Element Methods for Nonrigid Motion Analysis. In *Physics-Based Modelling in Computer Vision*, 1995. 8

S. Ilić and P. Fua. Using Dirichlet Free Form Deformation to Fit Deformable Models to Noisy 3D Data. In *European Conference on Computer Vision*, May 2002. DOI: 10.1007/3-540-47967-8_47 14

S. Ilić and P. Fua. Implicit Meshes for Surface Reconstruction. *IEEE Transactions on Pattern Analysis and Machine Intelligence*, 8(2):328–333, 2006. DOI: 10.1109/TPAMI.2006.37 14

S. Ilić and P. Fua. Non-Linear Beam Model for Tracking Large Deformation. In *International Conference on Computer Vision*, October 2007. DOI: 10.1109/ICCV.2007.4408947 8

S. Ilić, M. Salzmann, and P. Fua. Implicit Meshes for Effective Silhouette Handling. *International Journal of Computer Vision*, 72(7), 2007. DOI: 10.1007/s11263-006-8595-0 81

M. Irani. Multi-Frame Optical Flow Estimation Using Subspace Constraints. In *International Conference on Computer Vision*, 1999. DOI: 10.1109/ICCV.1999.791283 57

G. Irving, J. Teran, and R. Fedkiw. Invertible Finite Elements for Robust Simulation of Large Deformation. In *Symposium on Computer Animation*, 2004. DOI: 10.1145/1028523.1028541 7

D.L. James and D.K. Pai. Artdefo: Accurate Real Time Deformable Objects. In *ACM SIGGRAPH*, pages 65–72, 1999. DOI: 10.1145/311535.311542 7

N. Jojic and T.S. Huang. Estimating Cloth Draping Parameters from Range Data. In *Workshop on Synthetic-Natural Hybrid Coding and 3-D Imaging*, pages 73–76, 1997. 8

I. T. Jolliffe. *Principal Component Analysis*. Springer-Verlag, 1986. 10

F. Kahl. Multiple View Geometry and the L_∞-Norm. In *International Conference on Computer Vision*, pages 1002–1009, 2005. 30

F. Kahraman, M. Gokmen, S. Darkner, and R. Larsen. An active illumination and appearance (aia) model for face alignment. In *Conference on Computer Vision and Pattern Recognition*, 2007. DOI: 10.1109/CVPR.2007.383399 12

A. Kambhamettu, D. Goldgoff, D. Terzopoulos, and T.S. Huang. *Handbook of Pattern Recognition and Image Processing: Computer Vision*, chapter Non Rigid Motion Analysis, pages 405–430. Academic Press, 1994. 8

M. Kass, A. Witkin, and D. Terzopoulos. Snakes: Active Contour Models. *International Journal of Computer Vision*, 1(4):321–331, 1988. DOI: 10.1007/BF00133570 5, 8, 74

Q. Ke and T. Kanade. Quasiconvex Optimization for Robust Geometric Reconstruction. In *International Conference on Computer Vision*, pages 986–993, 2005. DOI: 10.1109/TPAMI.2007.1083 30

L. P. Kobbelt, T. Bareuther, and H. P. Seidel. Multiresolution Shape Deformations for Meshes With Dynamic Vertex Connectivity. In *Eurographics*, 2000. DOI: 10.1111/1467-8659.00417 14

L. P. Kobbelt. Sqrt(3)-Subdivision. In *ACM SIGGRAPH*, 2000. 14

D.J. Kriegman and P.N. Belhumeur. What Shadows Reveal About Object Structure. In *European Conference on Computer Vision*, pages 399–414, 1998. 18

V. Krishnamurthy and M. Levoy. Fitting Smooth Surfaces to Dense Polygon Meshes. In *ACM SIGGRAPH*, pages 313–324, 1996. DOI: 10.1145/237170.237270 14

N. D. Lawrence. Gaussian Process Models for Visualisation of High Dimensional Data. In *Neural Information Processing Systems*. MIT Press, 2004. 10

N. D. Lawrence. Learning for Larger Datasets With the Gaussian Process Latent Variable Model. In *International Workshop on Artificial Intelligence and Statistics*, 2007. 11

V. Lepetit and P. Fua. Keypoint Recognition Using Randomized Trees. *IEEE Transactions on Pattern Analysis and Machine Intelligence*, 28(9):1465–1479, September 2006. DOI: 10.1109/TPAMI.2006.188 19

J. Liang, D. Dementhon, and D. Doermann. Flattening Curved Documents in Images. In *Conference on Computer Vision and Pattern Recognition*, pages 338–345, 2005. DOI: 10.1109/CVPR.2005.163 34

X. Llado, A. Del Bue, and L. Agapito. Non-Rigid Metric Reconstruction from Perspective Cameras. *Image Vision Computing*, 28:1339–1353, 2010. DOI: 10.1016/j.imavis.2010.01.014 54, 56, 61, 74, 75

C. Loop. Smooth Subdivision Surfaces Based on Triangles. Master thesis, Department of Mathematics, University of Utah, 1987. 7, 14

D.G. Lowe. Distinctive Image Features from Scale-Invariant Keypoints. *International Journal of Computer Vision*, 20(2):91–110, 2004. DOI: 10.1023/B:VISI.0000029664.99615.94 19

B. Lucas and T. Kanade. An Iterative Image Registration Technique With an Application to Stereo Vision. In *International Joint Conference on Artificial Intelligence*, pages 674–679, 1981. 57

E. Malis and M. Vargas. Deeper Understanding of the Homography Decomposition for Vision-Based Control. Technical report, INRIA, 2007. 77

M. Marques and J. Costeira. Estimating 3D shape from degenerate sequences with missing data. *Computer Vision and Image Understanding*, 113(2):261–272, 2009. DOI: 10.1016/j.cviu.2008.09.004 57

I. Matthews and S. Baker. Active Appearance Models Revisited. *International Journal of Computer Vision*, 60:135–164, November 2004. DOI: 10.1023/B:VISI.0000029666.37597.d3 11

T. McInerney and D. Terzopoulos. A Finite Element Model for 3D Shape Reconstruction and Nonrigid Motion Tracking. In *International Conference on Computer Vision*, pages 518–523, 1993. DOI: 10.1109/ICCV.1993.378169 8

T. McInerney and D. Terzopoulos. A Dynamic Finite Element Surface Model for Segmentation and Tracking in Multidimensional Medical Images With Application to Cardiac 4D Image Analysis. *Computerized Medical Imaging and Graphics*, 19(1):69–83, 1995. DOI: 10.1016/0895-6111(94)00040-9 8

T. McInerney and D. Terzopoulos. Deformable Models in Medical Image Analysis: A Survey. *Medical Image Analysis*, 1:91–108, 1996. DOI: 10.1016/S1361-8415(96)80007-7 8

D. Metaxas and D. Terzopoulos. Constrained Deformable Superquadrics and Nonrigid Motion Tracking. *IEEE Transactions on Pattern Analysis and Machine Intelligence*, 15(6):580–591, 1993. DOI: 10.1109/34.216727 8

Microsoft. Kinect Camera, 2010. http://www.xbox.com:80/en-US/kinect/. 3

L. Moccozet and N. Magnenat-Thalmann. Dirichlet Free-Form Deformation and Their Application to Hand Simulation. In *Computer Animation*, 1997. 14

J. Montagnat, H. Delingette, and N. Ayache. A Review of Deformable Surfaces: Topology, Geometry and Deformation. *Image Vision Computing*, 19:1023–1040, 2001. DOI: 10.1016/S0262-8856(01)00064-6 8

F. Moreno-Noguer, M. Salzmann, V. Lepetit, and P. Fua. Capturing 3D Stretchable Surfaces from Single Images in Closed Form. In *Conference on Computer Vision and Pattern Recognition*, June 2009. DOI: 10.1109/CVPR.2009.5206758 38, 44, 81, 82

F. Moreno-Noguer, J. Porta, and P. Fua. Exploring Ambiguities for Monocular Non-Rigid Shape Estimation. In *European Conference on Computer Vision*, September 2010. DOI: 10.1007/978-3-642-15558-1_27 38, 82

M. Müller, J. Dorsey, L. McMillan, R. Jagnow, and B. Cutler. Stable Real-Time Deformations. In *ACM Symposium on Computer Animation*, pages 49–54, 2002. DOI: 10.1145/545261.545269 7

M. Müller, B. Heidelberger, M. Teschner, and M. Gross. Meshless Deformations based on Shape Matching. In *ACM SIGGRAPH*, pages 471–478, 2005. DOI: 10.1145/1073204.1073216 72

C. Nastar and N. Ayache. Frequency-Based Nonrigid Motion Analysis. *IEEE Transactions on Pattern Analysis and Machine Intelligence*, 18(11), November 1996. DOI: 10.1109/34.544076 9

C. Nastar, B. Moghaddam, and A. Pentland. Generalized Image Matching: Statistical Learning of Physically-Based Deformations. In *European Conference on Computer Vision*, pages 589–598, 1996. DOI: 10.1007/BFb0015569 12

S.K. Nayar, K. Ikeuchi, and T. Kanade. Shape from Interreflections. *International Journal of Computer Vision*, 6(3):173–195, 1991. DOI: 10.1007/BF00115695 18

H.N. Ng and R.L. Grimsdale. Computer Graphics Techniques for Modeling Cloth. *Computer Graphics and Applications*, 16(5):28–41, 1996. DOI: 10.1109/38.536273 7

S.I. Olsen and A. Bartoli. Implicit Non-Rigid Structure-from-Motion With Priors. *Journal of Mathematical Imaging and Vision*, 31:233–244, 2008. DOI: 10.1007/s10851-007-0060-3 57, 58, 63, 74

M. Oren and S.K. Nayar. A Theory of Specular Surface Geometry. *International Journal of Computer Vision*, 24(2):105–124, 1996. DOI: 10.1023/A:1007954719939 18

M. Paladini, A. Del Bue, S.M. Dodig, J. Xavier, and L. Agapito. Factorization for Non-Rigid and Articulated Structure using Metric Projections. In *Conference on Computer Vision and Pattern Recognition*, 2009. DOI: 10.1109/CVPR.2009.5206602 57

A. Pentland and S. Sclaroff. Closed-Form Solutions for Physically Based Shape Modeling and Recognition. *IEEE Transactions on Pattern Analysis and Machine Intelligence*, 13:715–729, 1991. DOI: 10.1109/34.85660 9

A. Pentland. Automatic Extraction of Deformable Part Models. *International Journal of Computer Vision*, 4(2):107–126, 1990. DOI: 10.1007/BF00127812 9

M. Perriollat and A. Bartoli. A Quasi-Minimal Model for Paper-Like Surfaces. In *BenCos: Workshop Towards Benchmarking Automated Calibration, Orientation and Surface Reconstruction from Images*, 2007. DOI: 10.1109/CVPR.2007.383356 34, 81

M. Perriollat, R. Hartley, and A. Bartoli. Monocular Template-Based Reconstruction of Inextensible Surfaces. *International Journal of Computer Vision*, 2010. DOI: 10.1007/s11263-010-0352-8 44, 45, 78, 79

J. Peyras, A. Bartoli, H. Mercier, and P. Dalle. Segmented AAMs Improve Person-Independent Face Fitting. In *British Machine Vision Conference*, 2007. 12

G. Picinbono, H. Delingette, and N. Ayache. Real-Time Large Displacement Elasticity for Surgery Simulation: Non-Linear Tensor-Mass Model. In *International Conference on Medical Robotics, Imaging And Computer Assisted Surgery*, pages 643–652, 2000. DOI: 10.1007/978-3-540-40899-4_66 7

J. Pilet, V. Lepetit, and P. Fua. Fast Non-Rigid Surface Detection, Registration and Realistic Augmentation. *International Journal of Computer Vision*, 76(2), February 2008. DOI: 10.1007/s11263-006-0017-9 2, 8, 19

D. Pizarro, J. Peyras, and A. Bartoli. Light-invariant fitting of active appearance models. In *Conference on Computer Vision and Pattern Recognition*, 2008. DOI: 10.1109/CVPR.2008.4587651 12

V. Rabaud and S. Belongie. Re-Thinking Non-Rigid Structure from Motion. In *Conference on Computer Vision and Pattern Recognition*, June 2008. DOI: 10.1109/CVPR.2008.4587679 62, 63, 71, 72, 74

V. Rabaud and S. Belongie. Linear Embeddings in Non-Rigid Structure from Motion. In *Conference on Computer Vision and Pattern Recognition*, June 2009. DOI: 10.1109/CVPR.2009.5206628 62, 63, 64

S. Romdhani and T. Vetter. Efficient, Robust and Accurate Fitting of a 3D Morphable Model. In *International Conference on Computer Vision*, 2003. DOI: 10.1109/ICCV.2003.1238314 12, 40

S. Roweis and L. Saul. Nonlinear Dimensionality Reduction by Locally Linear Embedding. *Science*, 290(5500):2323–2326, 2000. DOI: 10.1126/science.290.5500.2323 10

M. Salzmann and P. Fua. Linear Local Models for Monocular Reconstruction of Deformable Surfaces. *IEEE Transactions on Pattern Analysis and Machine Intelligence*, 2011. DOI: 10.1109/TPAMI.2010.158 40, 42, 43, 44, 45, 46, 48

M. Salzmann and R. Urtasun. Combining discriminative and generative methods for 3d deformable surface and articulated pose reconstruction. In *Conference on Computer Vision and Pattern Recognition*, San Francisco, CA, June 2010. DOI: 10.1109/CVPR.2010.5540155 49

M. Salzmann, R. Hartley, and P. Fua. Convex Optimization for Deformable Surface 3D Tracking. In *International Conference on Computer Vision*, October 2007. DOI: 10.1109/ICCV.2007.4409031 30, 31, 32, 33

M. Salzmann, V. Lepetit, and P. Fua. Deformable Surface Tracking Ambiguities. In *Conference on Computer Vision and Pattern Recognition*, June 2007. DOI: 10.1109/CVPR.2007.383238 17, 30

M. Salzmann, J. Pilet, S. Ilić, and P. Fua. Surface Deformation Models for Non-Rigid 3D Shape Recovery. *IEEE Transactions on Pattern Analysis and Machine Intelligence*, 29(8):1481–1487, February 2007. DOI: 10.1109/TPAMI.2007.1080 35, 52

M. Salzmann, F. Moreno-Noguer, V. Lepetit, and P. Fua. Closed-Form Solution to Non-Rigid 3D Surface Registration. In *European Conference on Computer Vision*, October 2008. DOI: 10.1007/978-3-540-88693-8_43 36, 37, 43, 44, 45, 46, 79, 81

M. Salzmann, R. Urtasun, and P. Fua. Local Deformation Models for Monocular 3D Shape Recovery. In *Conference on Computer Vision and Pattern Recognition*, June 2008. DOI: 10.1109/CVPR.2008.4587499 13, 40, 46

M. Salzmann. *Learning and Recovering 3D Surface Deformations*. PhD thesis, Ecole Polytechnique Fédérale de Lausanne, 2009. 35

J. Sanchez-Riera, J. Ostlund, P. Fua, and F. Moreno-Noguer. Simultaneous Pose, Correspondence and Non-Rigid Shape. In *Conference on Computer Vision and Pattern Recognition*, June 2010. DOI: 10.1109/CVPR.2010.5539831 43

B. Schoelkopf, C.J.C. Burges, and A.J. Smola. Advances in Kernel Methods. In *Support Vector Learning*. MIT Press, 1999. 10

T.W. Sederberg and S.R. Parry. Free-Form Deformation of Solid Geometric Models. *ACM SIGGRAPH*, 20(4), 1986. DOI: 10.1109/CVPRW.2008.4563071 14

A. Shaji and S. Chandran. Riemannian Manifold Optimisation for Non-Rigid Structure from Motion. In *Conference on Computer Vision and Pattern Recognition*, 2008. DOI: 10.1145/15922.15903 58, 61, 62

A. Shaji, A. Varol, L. Torresani, and P. Fua. Simultaneous Point Matching and 3D Deformable Surface Reconstruction. In *Conference on Computer Vision and Pattern Recognition*, June 2010. DOI: 10.1109/CVPR.2010.5539827 42, 43

S. Shen, W. Shi, and Y. Liu. Monocular 3D Tracking of Inextensible Deformable Surfaces Under L2-Norm. In *Asian Conference on Computer Vision*, 2009. DOI: 10.1109/TIP.2009.2038115 48

K. Sim and R. Hartley. Removing Outliers Using the L_∞ Norm. In *Conference on Computer Vision and Pattern Recognition*, pages 485–494, 2006. DOI: 10.1109/CVPR.2006.253 31

O. Sorkine, D. Cohen-Or, Y. Lipman, M. Alexa, C. Rössl, and H.-P. Seidel. Laplacian Surface Editing. In *Symposium on Geometry Processing*, pages 175–184, 2004. DOI: 10.1145/1057432.1057456 14

J. Starck and A. Hilton. Spherical Matching for Temporal Correspondence of Non-Rigid Surfaces. In *International Conference on Computer Vision*, pages 1387–1394, 2005. DOI: 10.1109/ICCV.2005.229 2

J. Starck and A. Hilton. Correspondence Labelling for Wide-Timeframe Free-Form Surface Matching. In *International Conference on Computer Vision*, 2007. DOI: 10.1109/ICCV.2007.4409108 2

J.F. Sturm. Using SeDuMi 1.02, a MATLAB toolbox for optimization over symmetric cones, 1999. 31, 44, 46

S. Sullivan, L. Sandford, and J. Ponce. Using Geometric Distance Fits for 3D Object Modeling and Recognition. *IEEE Transactions on Pattern Analysis and Machine Intelligence*, 16(12):1183–1196, December 1994. DOI: 10.1109/34.387489 81

R. Szeliski and R. Weiss. Robust Shape Recovery from Occluding Contours Using a Linear Smoother. *International Journal of Computer Vision*, 28(1):27–44, 1998. DOI: 10.1023/A:1008050630628 81

H. Tao and T.S. Huang. Connected Vibrations: A Modal Analysis Approach for Non-Rigid Motion Tracking. In *Conference on Computer Vision and Pattern Recognition*, 1998. DOI: 10.1109/CVPR.1998.698685 9

J. Taylor, A. D. Jepson, and K. N. Kutulakos. Non-Rigid Structure from Locally-Rigid Motion. In *Conference on Computer Vision and Pattern Recognition*, June 2010. DOI: 10.1109/CVPR.2010.5540002 76, 78

J.B. Tenenbaum, V. de Silva, and J.C. Langford. A Global Geometric Framework for Nonlinear Dimensionality Reduction. *Science*, 290(5500):2319–2323, 2000. DOI: 10.1126/science.290.5500.2319 10

D. Terzopoulos and D. Metaxas. Dynamic 3D Models With Local and Global Deformations: Deformable Superquadrics. *IEEE Transactions on Pattern Analysis and Machine Intelligence*, 13:703–714, 1991. DOI: 10.1109/34.85659 8

D. Terzopoulos, J. Platt, A. Barr, and K. Fleicher. Elastically Deformable Models. *ACM SIGGRAPH*, 21(4):205–214, 1987. DOI: 10.1145/37402.37427 5

D. Terzopoulos, A. Witkin, and M. Kass. Constraints on Deformable Models: Recovering 3D Shape and Nongrid Motion. *Artificial Intelligence*, 36(1):91–123, 1988. DOI: 10.1016/0004-3702(88)90080-X 5

M.E. Tipping and C.M. Bishop. Probabilistic Principal Component Anlaysis. *Journal of the Royal Statistical Society, B*, 6(3):611–622, 1999. 10, 41, 70

C. Tomasi and T. Kanade. Shape and Motion from Image Streams Under Orthography: A Factorization Method. *International Journal of Computer Vision*, 9(2):137–154, 1992. DOI: 10.1007/BF00129684 51, 53, 56, 60, 63

L. Torresani, D. B. Yang, E. J. Alexander, and C. Bregler. Tracking and Modeling Non-Rigid Objects With Rank Constraints. In *Conference on Computer Vision and Pattern Recognition*, pages 493–500, 2001. DOI: 10.1109/CVPR.2001.990515 57, 61, 74

L. Torresani, A. Hertzmann, and C. Bregler. Learning Non-Rigid 3D Shape from 2D Motion. In *Neural Information Processing Systems*. MIT Press, 2003. 57

L. Torresani, A. Hertzmann, and C. Bregler. Nonrigid Structure-From-Motion: Estimating Shape and Motion With Hierarchical Priors. *IEEE Transactions on Pattern Analysis and Machine Intelligence*, 30(5):878–892, 2008. DOI: 10.1109/TPAMI.2007.70752 61, 62, 64, 65, 69, 70, 71, 72, 73

L.V. Tsap, D.B. Goldgof, S. Sarkar, and W.C. Huang. Efficient Nonlinear Finite Element Modeling of Nonrigid Objects Via Optimization of Mesh Models. *Computer Vision and Image Understanding*, 69(3):330–350, March 1998. DOI: 10.1006/cviu.1998.0663 8

L.V. Tsap, D.B. Goldgof, and S. Sarkar. Nonrigid Motion Analysis Based on Dynamic Refinement of Finite Element Models. *IEEE Transactions on Pattern Analysis and Machine Intelligence*, 22(5):526–543, 2000. DOI: 10.1109/34.857007 8

S. Ullman. Maximizing rigidity: The incremental recovery of 3-d structure from rigid and rubbery motion. *Perception*, 13:255–274, 1983. DOI: 10.1068/p130255 51, 79

R. Urtasun, D. Fleet, A. Hertzman, and P. Fua. Priors for People Tracking from Small Training Sets. In *International Conference on Computer Vision*, October 2005. DOI: 10.1109/ICCV.2005.193 12

R. Urtasun, D. Fleet, and P. Fua. 3D People Tracking With Gaussian Process Dynamical Models. In *Conference on Computer Vision and Pattern Recognition*, 2006. DOI: 10.1109/CVPR.2006.15 12

A. Varol, M. Salzmann, E. Tola, and P. Fua. Template-Free Monocular Reconstruction of Deformable Surfaces. In *International Conference on Computer Vision*, September 2009. DOI: 10.1109/ICCV.2009.5459403 76, 77, 78

R. Vidal and D. Abretske. Nonrigid Shape and Motion from Multiple Perspective Views. In *European Conference on Computer Vision*, 2006. DOI: 10.1007/11744047_16 54

P. Volino and N. Magnenat-Thalmann. Comparing Efficiency of Integration Methods for Cloth Simulation. In *Computer Graphics International*, pages 265–274, 2001. DOI: 10.1109/CGI.2001.934683 7

P. Volino, M. Courchesne, and N. Magnenat-Thalmann. Versatile and Efficient Techniques for Simulating Cloth and Other Deformable Objects. In *ACM SIGGRAPH*, pages 137–144, August 1995. DOI: 10.1145/218380.218432 7

G. Wang and Q.M. Wu. Quasi-perspective Projection Model: Theory and Application to Structure and Motion Factorization from Uncalibrated Image Sequences. *International Journal of Computer Vision*, 87(3):213–234, 2010. DOI: 10.1007/s11263-009-0267-4 54

J.M. Wang, D.J. Fleet, and A. Hertzmann. Gaussian Process Dynamical Models. In *Neural Information Processing Systems*, 2005. 11

G. Wang, H.T. Tsui, and Q.M. Wu. Rotation constrained power factorization for structure from motion of nonrigid objects. *Pattern Recognition Letters*, 29:72–80, 2008. DOI: 10.1016/j.patrec.2007.09.004 58

K. Q. Weinberger and L. K. Saul. Unsupervised Learning of Image Manifolds by Semidefinite Programming. In *Conference on Computer Vision and Pattern Recognition*, June 2004. DOI: 10.1109/CVPR.2004.1315272 10

W. Welch and A. Witkin. Free-Form Shape Design Using Triangulated Surfaces. In *ACM SIGGRAPH*, pages 247–256, 1994. DOI: 10.1145/192161.192216 14

R. White and D.A. Forsyth. Combining Cues: Shape from Shading and Texture. In *Conference on Computer Vision and Pattern Recognition*, 2006. DOI: 10.1109/CVPR.2006.79 39, 82

R. White, K. Crane, and D.A. Forsyth. Capturing and Animating Occluded Cloth. In *ACM SIGGRAPH*, 2007. DOI: 10.1145/1276377.1276420 2

R.J. Woodham. Photometric Method for Determining Surface Orientation from Multiple Images. *Optical Engineering*, 19(1):139–144, January 1980. 3

X. Wu, Michael S. Downes, Tolga Goktekin, and Frank Tendick. Adaptive Nonlinear Finite Elements for Deformable Body Simulation Using Dynamic Progressive Meshes. In *Computer Graphics Forum*, pages 349–358, 2001. DOI: 10.1111/1467-8659.00527 7

J. Xiao and T. Kanade. Non-Rigid Shape and Motion Recovery: Degenerate Deformations. In *Conference on Computer Vision and Pattern Recognition*, pages 668–675, 2004. DOI: 10.1109/CVPR.2004.176 56

J. Xiao and T. Kanade. Uncalibrated Perspective Reconstruction of Deformable Structures. In *International Conference on Computer Vision*, 2005. DOI: 10.1109/ICCV.2005.241 52, 54, 56, 67, 68

J. Xiao, S. Baker, I. Matthews, and T. Kanade. Real-Time Combined 2D+3D Active Appearance Models. In *Conference on Computer Vision and Pattern Recognition*, pages 535–542, 2004. DOI: 10.1109/CVPR.2004.1315210 12

J Xiao, J.-X. Chai, and T. Kanade. A Closed-Form Solution to Non-Rigid Shape and Motion Recovery. In *European Conference on Computer Vision*, pages 573–587, 2004. DOI: 10.1007/978-3-540-24673-2_46 56, 60, 64, 65, 67, 68, 69, 70

Z. Zhang and A.R. Hanson. Scaled Euclidean 3D Reconstruction Based on Externally Uncalibrated Cameras. In *IEEE Symposium on Computer Vision*, pages 37–42, 1995. DOI: 10.1109/ISCV.1995.476974 77

Z. Zhang, C. Tan, and L. Fan. Restoration of Curved Document Images Through 3D Shape Modeling. In *Conference on Computer Vision and Pattern Recognition*, June 2004. DOI: 10.1109/CVPR.2004.210 34, 82

K. Zhou, J. Huang, J. Snyder, X. Liu, H. Bao, B. Guo, and H.-Y. Shum. Large Mesh Deformation Using the Volumetric Graph Laplacian. *ACM SIGGRAPH*, 24(3):496–503, 2005. DOI: 10.1145/1073204.1073219 14

J. Zhu, S. Hoi, C. Steven, Z. Xu, and M.R. Lyu. An Effective Approach to 3D Deformable Surface Tracking. In *European Conference on Computer Vision*, pages 766–779, 2008. DOI: 10.1007/978-3-540-88690-7_57 32, 33

S. Zhu, L. Zhang, and B.M. Smith. Model Evolution: An Incremental Approach to Non-Rigid Structure from Motion. In *Conference on Computer Vision and Pattern Recognition*, June 2010. DOI: 10.1109/CVPR.2010.5540085 58, 63, 68, 74

O.C. Zienkiewicz. *The Finite Element Method*. McGraw-Hill, 1989. 5, 6

D. Zorin, P. Schröder, and W. Sweldens. Interactive Multiresolution Mesh Editing. In *ACM SIGGRAPH*, pages 259–268, 1997. DOI: 10.1145/258734.258863 14

Authors' Biographies

MATHIEU SALZMANN

Mathieu Salzmann received his B.Sc and M.Sc degrees in computer science in 2004 from EPFL (Swiss Federal Institute of Technology). He obtained his PhD degree in computer vision in 2009 from EPFL. He then joined the International Computer Science Institute and the EECS departement at UC Berkeley as a postdoctoral fellow. Recently, he joined TTI Chicago as a Research Assistant Professor. His research interests include non-rigid shape recovery, human pose estimation, and optimization techniques for computer vision.

PASCAL FUA

Pascal Fua received an engineering degree from École Polytechnique, Paris, in 1984 and the Ph.D. degree in Computer Science from the University of Orsay in 1989. He joined EPFL (Swiss Federal Institute of Technology) in 1996 where he is now a Professor in the School of Computer and Communication Science. Before that, he worked at SRI International and at INRIA Sophia-Antipolis as a Computer Scientist. His research interests include shape modeling and motion recovery from images, analysis of microscopy images, and Augmented Reality. He has (co)authored over 150 publications in refereed journals and conferences. He has been an associate editor of IEEE journal Transactions for Pattern Analysis and Machine Intelligence and has often been a program committee member, area chair, and program chair of major vision conferences.

Printed in the United States
by Baker & Taylor Publisher Services